Contents

Introduction

For many, the buckaroo in the ten-gallon hat represents a time gone by. But the American cowboy is still alive and well. Across the West, real ranches, rodeos, and cattle drives aren't just preserving the frontier spirit—they're actively practicing it.

With this in mind, we've gathered some of the best cowboy projects from our archive, including a snowman, rooster, Santa, and more. They range in difficulty from beginner to advanced—so whether you're new to carving or have been at it for years, we've got you covered. We've also included tips and techniques from today's leading caricature carvers, such as Dave Stetson, Chris Hammack, and Dale Green, to help those woodchips fly.

So, sit back, kick up your heels, and enjoy bringing these classic characters to life. You might even see a tumbleweed roll by.

Happy carving!
The *Woodcarving Illustrated* team

Little Hombre

Rustle up this Western caricature with just two tools

By Dave Stetson
Photography by Roger Schroeder

With an oversized head, straightforward pose, and exceptionally long feet, this cowboy is a great project for beginners.

Using only two tools and a chunk of basswood, I can carve him in thirty minutes, with four of those minutes set aside for a coffee break.

Getting Started

Transfer the profile pattern to the blank using your preferred method (I sketched mine on with a pencil), and use a scroll saw or coping saw to cut the rough shape. Draw vertical centerlines on the front and back of the blank.

> **TIP**
>
> **IRONING OUT THE WRINKLES**
>
> *On caricatures and realistic figures, wrinkles are typically made with V-cuts on the insides of arms and the backs of legs. Often overlooked is the fabric opposite the crease-producing joint of the arm or leg. The wrinkles in the crook will probably be prominent, but material tightens up on the opposite side. Create this stretched fabric look with a few flat-plane knife cuts.*

ROUGHING OUT

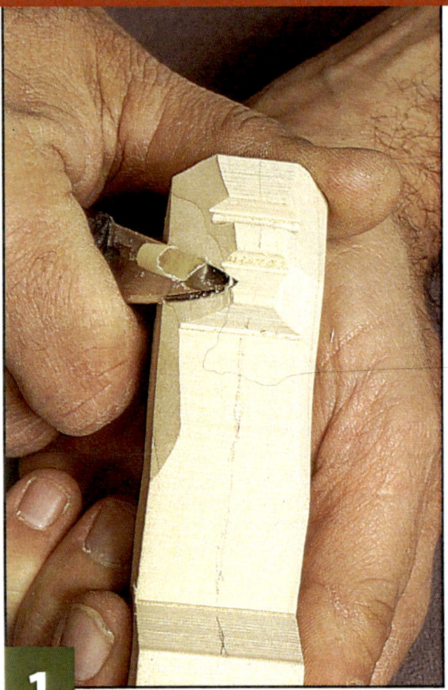

1 Remove the sharp corners. Remove excess wood from the front edges with a knife, working from the top down. Make a stop cut at the back of the base where the feet make contact and remove wood down to the stop cut at an angle.

2 Draw the basic landmarks. Make a continuous line to separate the head from the hat brim and the arm from the body. Stop the line where the hand enters the pocket. Repeat on the opposite side.

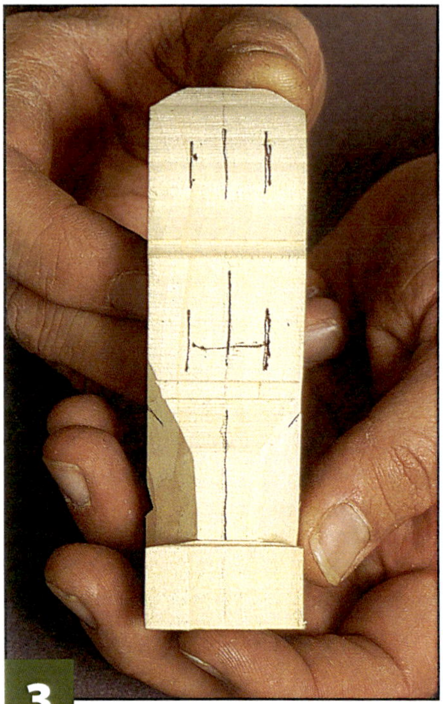

3 Divide the block. On the back of the blank, divide each side of the centerline in half to mark the width of the arms and the width of the brim and crown.

4 Separate the arms from the body. Use a ⅜" (10mm) 60° V-tool to carve along the lines made in Step 2 and to separate the hat brim and crown.

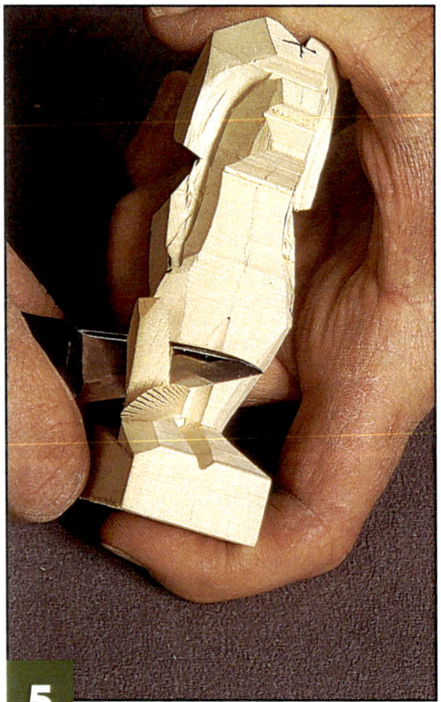

5 Shape and separate the legs and feet. Carve along the centerline between the legs using the same V-tool. Make beveled cuts with the knife on the front of the legs. Then separate the hat brim. Use the knife to remove wood underneath, making a tapering cut.

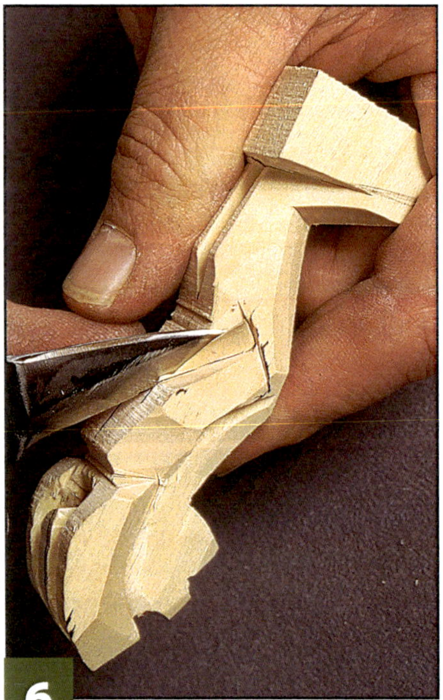

6 Define the arms. Make stop cuts behind the arms and remove wood up to the cuts, creating separation between the arms and the back.

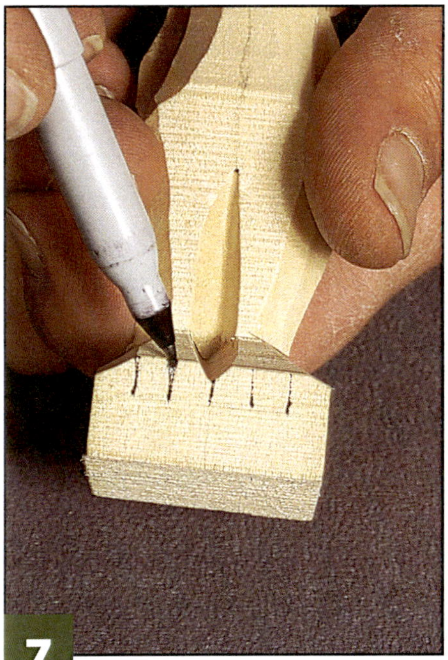

7 **Separate the feet.** Use a pen to divide the front of each boot into thirds. The inside third is where the tip of the boot will be located. Make stop cuts and remove wedges of wood from the outer lines to make the boots pointed.

CARVING THE FACE

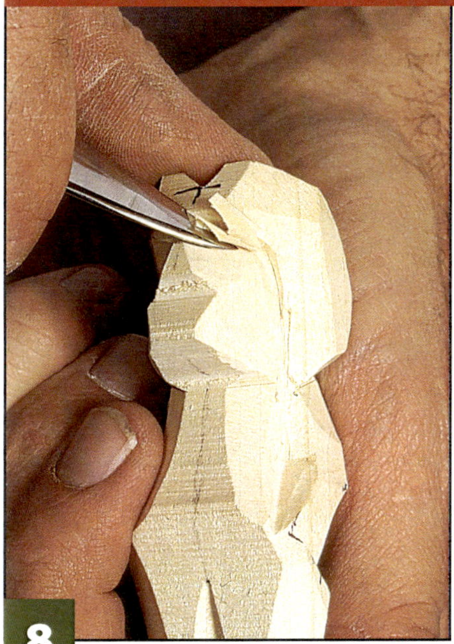

8 **Shape the nose.** Define it with a tapering cut right up to the hat brim. Then carve the nose, making sure half of it sticks out from the face and the rest is cut back into the face.

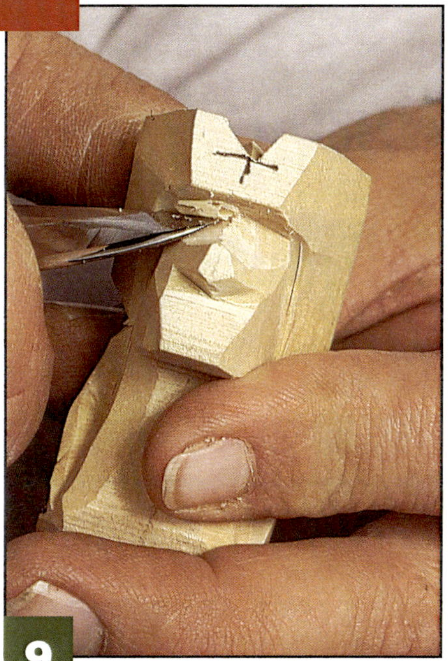

9 **Locate the eyes.** The eyes are not represented by mounds but instead by fairly flat planes carved on the face. Use a knife to create two symmetrical flat planes between the nose and the hat brim. Draw the mouth. Then sketch the smile lines that divide the cheeks from the dental mound.

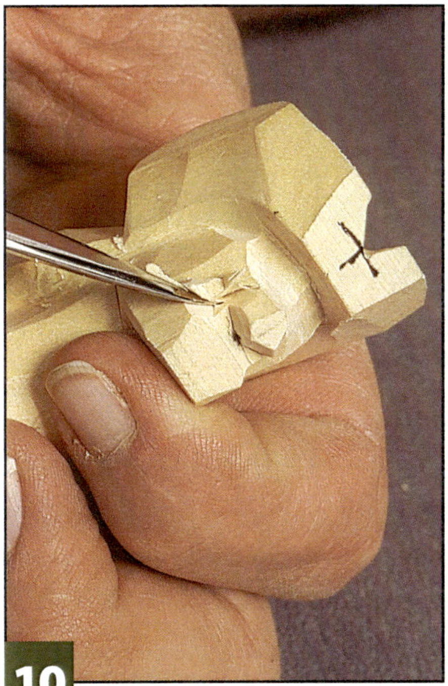

10 **Carve the mouth.** Place the point of the knife perpendicular to the face and make a stop cut along the smile line. Avoid cutting behind the nose. Then remove a wedge of wood on both sides of the stop cut. Remove a triangle of wood to reveal the flare of the nostril. Repeat on the opposite side.

ADDING DETAILS

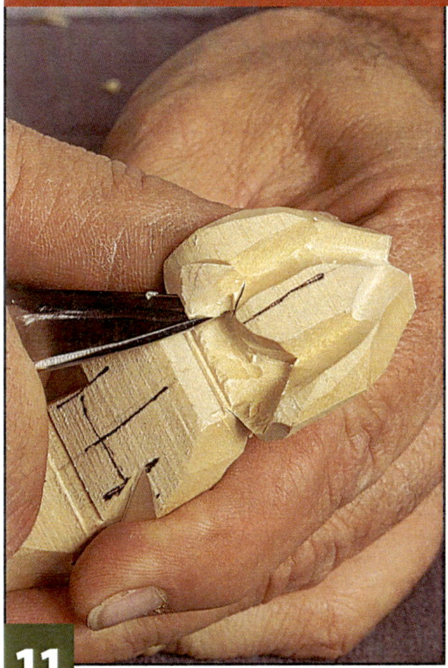

11 **Shape the hat.** Turn the figure over and carve two V-shaped chips of wood from the bottom of the back of the hat. This will create the illusion that the brim is curled up on its sides.

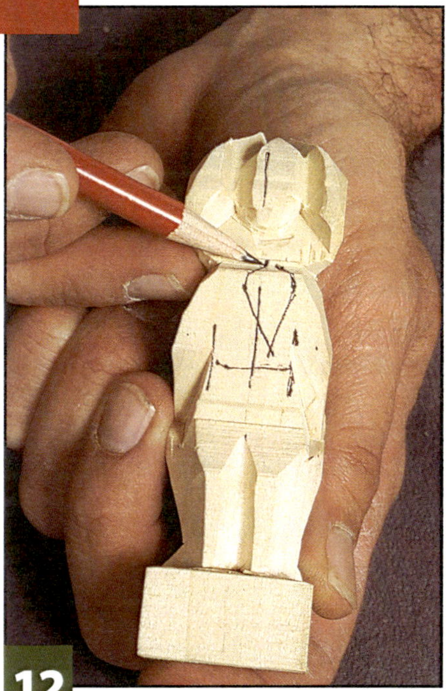

12 **Draw details.** Mark the bandana on the front and the strands of hair hanging from under the hat. On the rear of the cowboy, mark the bandana points, the vest, and the belt.

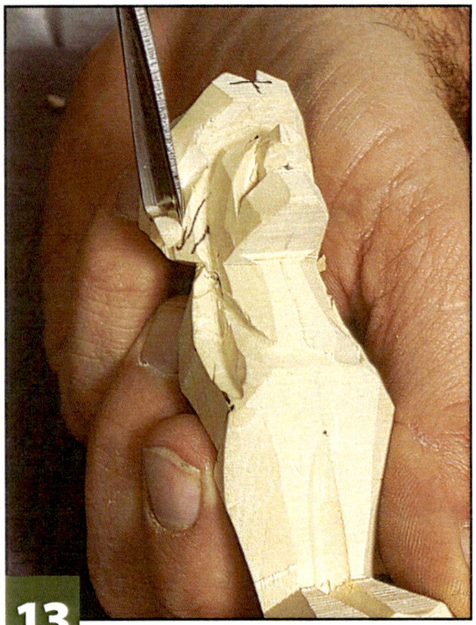

13 **Carve the front details.** Block in the bandana on the front with the ⅜" (10mm) 60° V-tool. Then separate the hair from the hat. On the rear, block in the bandana ends and separate them.

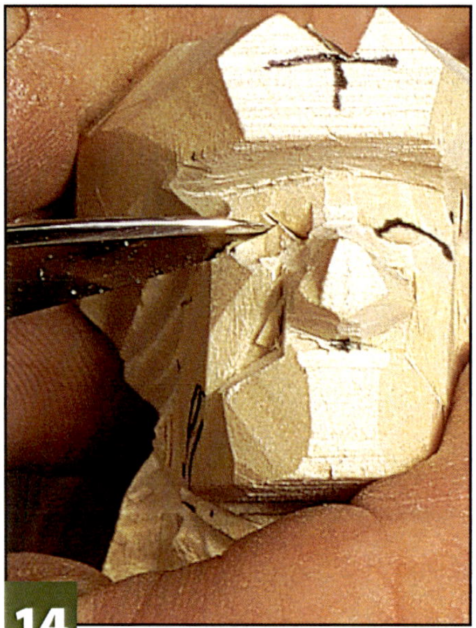

14 **Define the eyes.** Make a stop cut angling up and away from the inside corner of the eye for one-third the width of the eye. Then make a second cut angling down from the first cut to the outside corner of the eye. Repeat these two cuts to define the top of the other eye.

15 **Finish the eyes.** Make a relief cut from below, cutting up to the first two cuts to remove a wedge of wood. Repeat for the other eye. Make crow's feet by taking out wedges of wood at the outside corner of each eye.

PAINTING & FINISHING

16 **Add hair texture.** Using the ⅜" (10mm) 60° V-tool, carve strands of hair on the head and mustache. *Note: Hair is defined by the wood left between cuts, not by the cuts themselves.*

17 **Carve shirt wrinkles.** Remove wedges of wood in the crook of each arm to represent creases in the shirtsleeves. Carve a flat plane on the outside of each elbow to show that the shirt is being pulled taut.

18 **Define the back of the legs.** Remove a triangle of wood to define the bottom of the buttocks. Use the ⅜" (10mm) 60° V-tool to make creases at the backs of the knees. Then remove wood to shape the backs of the thighs. Use V-cuts to define the seam area in front. Scoop away some wood on the front of the pants to give definition to the pockets and the bend in the legs.

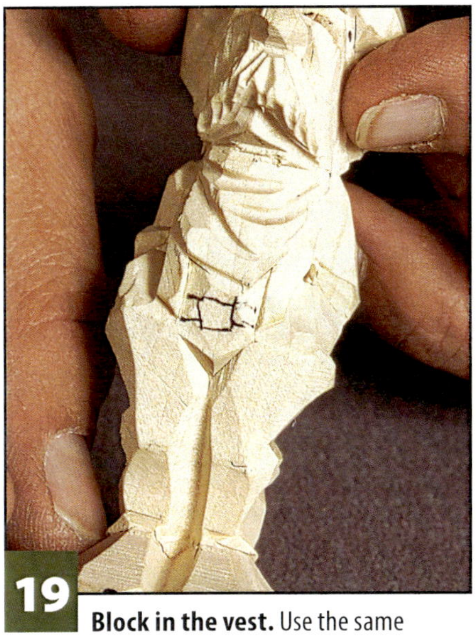

19 **Block in the vest.** Use the same V-tool to shape the vest. Draw the belt, and then use a stop cut to separate the belt from the shirt and pants.

20 **Detail the head.** Carve away wood to set the head back under the hat brim.

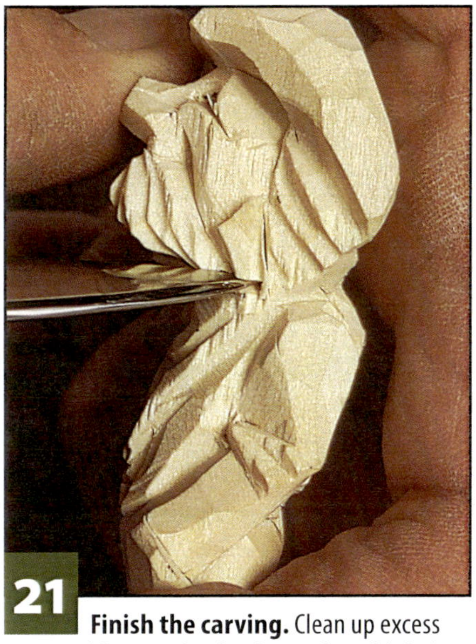

21 **Finish the carving.** Clean up excess wood from under the chin and establish the shape of the jaw by removing wood up to the hair. Open the nostrils using the point of the knife. Carve a slight bevel on the sides of the base. Add two coats of matte spray lacquer, and let dry before painting.

Little Hombre Patterns

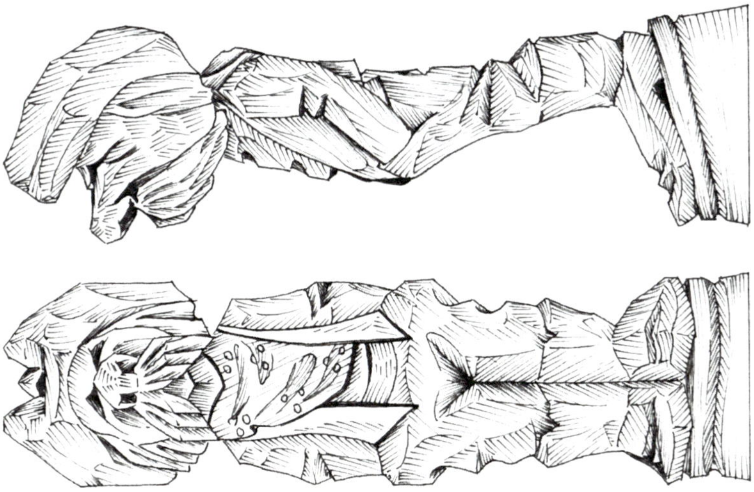

Paint Notes

Hat: black (2)

Vest: sandstone (2)

Flesh: medium flesh (2)

Hair, mustache: Quaker gray (2) drybrushed with antique white (2)

Bandana: tomato spice (2) shaded with black plum (1)

Shirt: timberline green (2)

Belt: burnt sienna (2)

Pants: burnt umber (2)

Boots: charcoal gray (1)

Base: sandstone (2)

1 DecoArt Americana
2 Delta Ceramcoat

materials & **tools**

MATERIALS

- Basswood: 1¹⁄₁₆" (2.7cm) thick, 1¼" x 4" (3.2cm x 10.2cm)
- Pen
- Acrylic paints, such as DecoArt Americana: black plum, charcoal gray; Delta Ceramcoat: antique white, black, burnt sienna, burnt umber, Quaker gray, medium flesh, sandstone, timberline green, tomato spice
- Finish, such as matte spray lacquer

TOOLS

- Scroll saw or coping saw
- Carving knife
- V-tool: ⅜" (10mm) 60°
- Paintbrushes: assorted

The author used these products for the project. Substitute your choice of brands, tools, and materials as desired.

A founding member of the Caricature Carvers of America, Dave Stetson has been carving since the early 1980s. Dave is a popular instructor who teaches carving classes across the United States. He lives in Scottsdale, Ariz. Contact Dave at stetsoncarving.com.

Rowdy the Roustabout

Hike up your trousers and get ready to carve this "out of control" character

By Dale Green

Cowboys don't change much as they age. Their hair gets a little grayer, they start wearing glasses, and they hitch up their pants a little higher—but they're always ready for action. "Rowdy" has decided not to let his advancing age get him down!

Getting Started

Transfer the front and side view patterns to the blank. Use a band saw to cut one outline. Tape the waste back in place, rotate the piece, and cut the second view. Draw a centerline on the front and add the major landmarks, such as the hat brim, belt buckle, hands, arms, and the bottoms of the pant legs. Remove some of the excess wood around these major landmarks.

ROUGHING OUT

1 **Draw two lines to establish the width of the face.** Then draw a line on each side to establish the depth of the face, and remove the excess wood with a carving knife. Draw the nose and chin, and then remove the surrounding wood. Draw the sideburns and ears. Block in the belt buckle.

2

Carve the outlines of the sideburns and ears. Then use the knife to carve the angle of the nose and forehead. As you carve, add the curve to the underside of the hat brim. Draw the placement of the arms and hands with the belt passing through the hands on both sides.

3

Carve the arms, hands, and belt. Use a 3/8" (10mm) 30° V-tool and the knife. Use the knife to shape the legs and establish the length of the pant legs. Carve one boot to its final size, adding the sole and heel details. Add the wrinkles in the boot.

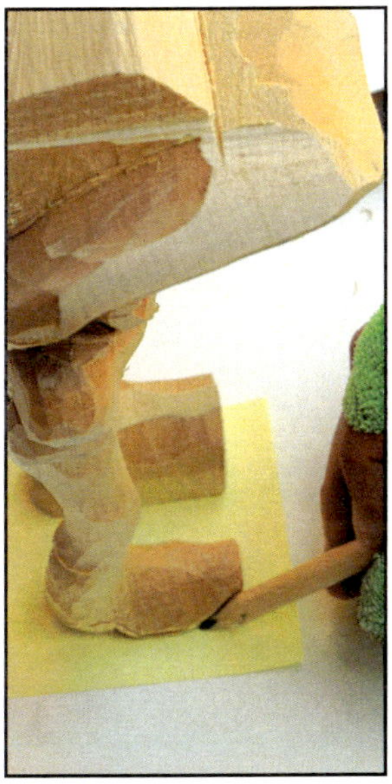

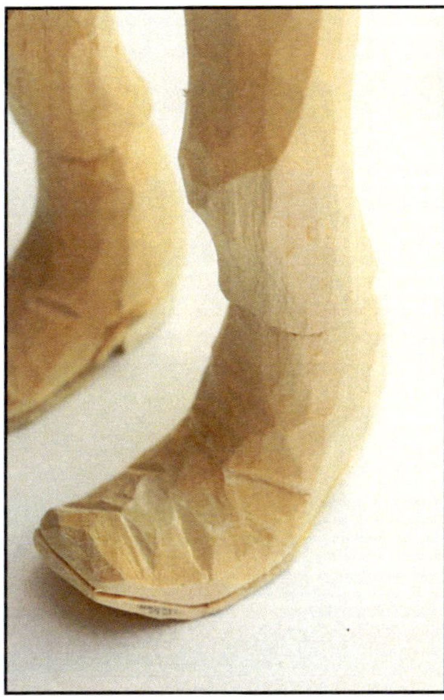

4

Carve the boots. Trace the completed boot onto heavy paper. Cut along the traced line. Flip the pattern over (so you don't end up carving two left feet) and trace it onto the bottom of the other foot. This way, you'll carve two boots that are the same size. Shape the other boot and leg to match the one you already carved.

5

Draw the lines for the eye sockets. Make a stop cut on the line with the knife and remove a wedge of wood up to the stop cut. Draw the brow line, and use the tip of the knife to make a stop cut along the line. Remove the wood up to the stop cut. Repeat for the other eye.

6 **Draw the eyelids.** Make stop cuts along the lines with the tip of the knife. Carve down the eyeballs between the stop cuts, and carve the pupils. Carve the wings of the nose, and establish the smile lines on both sides of the face. Round the edges of the smile lines to create jowls. Remove a triangle of wood on each side of the face between the wing of the nose and the smile line. Use the knife. This brings the nose out of the face.

7 **Round the mouth and chin.** Use the knife. Use the tip of the knife to carve the nostrils. Use a 1/8" (3mm) 30° V-tool to add hair texture, wrinkles, and eyebrows. Hollow the centers of the ears with the knife. Draw the collar and shirt details.

8 **Carve the mouth.** Draw the line between the lips. Make a stop cut on the line with the tip of the knife. Remove wood from under the stop cut to create the upper lip. Shape the chin with the knife. Use the knife to carve the collar and shirt button.

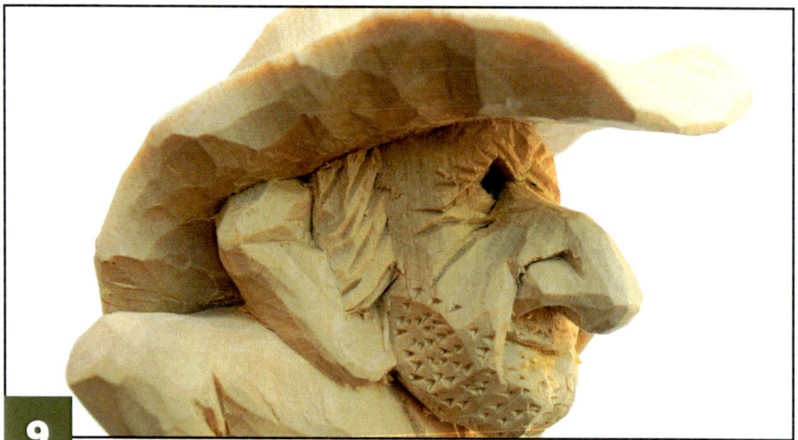

9 **Add the facial hair texture and hat details.** Use the 1/8" (3mm) 30° V-tool to lightly stab in a five-o'clock shadow around the cheeks, jaw, and upper lip. Use the knife to carve the hat details and to add cuffs to the shirtsleeves. Make sure the head is the same shape as the top of the hat. Then carve the top and bottom of the hat brim, adding some wrinkles to give it a weathered look. *Note: Don't let the brim get too thin.*

10 **Add the seam lines, fly, and pockets to the pants.** Use the 1/8" (3mm) 30° V-tool. Use a woodburner with a small skew nib to add the stitching to each boot. Use a small writing nib to burn the words on the belt buckle.

Making Glasses

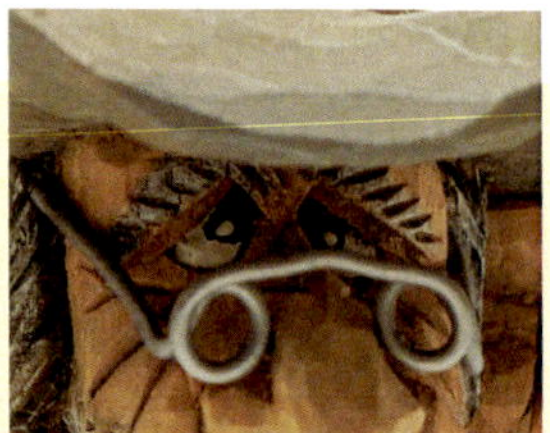

Use a 5" (12.7cm)-long piece of 12 gauge craft wire for the frames and sidepieces. I used 1/16" (2mm)-diameter armature wire. Wrap about a third of the length around a 3/16" (5mm)-diameter dowel. Allow enough space between the wraps for the bridge of the nose, and then wrap it around another dowel. Use a drill bit the same diameter as the wire and drill a hole into each sideburn. Cut the sidepieces to length. Perch the glasses close to the end of Rowdy's nose, insert the sidepieces into the holes in the sideburns, and glue them in place.

Painting and Finishing

Wash the carving with Simple Green® cleaner or dish soap and water. Scrub it with a denture brush to remove pencil marks, handprints, and any other dirt. Allow it to dry completely. Use a sponge brush to apply an even coat of Watco natural Danish oil to seal the entire carving. Let the oil dry for 24 hours, and then wipe off the excess with a soft cloth or paper towels. *Note: Sealing the carving allows you to apply a smooth coat of paint even on tough spots, such as the end grain.*

For this carving, I diluted acrylic paint heavily with water to create a wash. In general, mix 1 drop of paint with 10 drops of water. Colors that are more transparent, such as white, require less water. Paint the carving, using the photos and paint list as guides. Let the carving dry for at least 24 hours so the paint can cure.

To create an antiquing solution, add a pea-sized dab of burnt umber oil paint to 1 cup of boiled linseed oil, and mix until the paint is dissolved. Use a sponge brush to apply an even coat of the antiquing solution to the entire carving. Wait two or three minutes, and then blot off the excess with a soft cloth or paper towel. *Note: Dispose of the cloth or paper towels appropriately; BLO-soaked paper towels and rags can spontaneously combust.* Allow the carving to dry fully, and then apply two coats of Krylon® matte spray finish.

Paint Notes

Hatband, belt: raw umber (2)

Hat: mudstone (1)

Face: 1 drop medium flesh (1), 2 drops natural beige (3)

Hair, five-o'clock shadow: charcoal (1), drybrushed with titanium white (2)

Shirt, basecoat: 2 drops Napa red (2), 1 drop raw umber (2)

Shirt, plaid stripes: 2 drops olive green (3), 1 drop raw umber (2); yellow ochre (2)

Pants: 2 drops denim (1), 1 drop midnight blue (1)

Boots, upper section: very light wash of raw umber (2)

Boots, lower section: raw sienna (1)

Boot sole: raw umber (2)

1 Delta Ceramcoat
2 DecoArt Americana
3 Craftsmart

TIPS

PAINTING TIPS

- *When I get ready to seal my finished carving, I also seal a scrap piece of wood so I can test different colors. It's better to experiment with color on scrap wood than on your project.*
- *For Rowdy's five-o'clock shadow, thin the paint until it is mostly water, and then apply several coats until you get the desired result. This color will not be as dark as the sideburns.*
- *Keep a painting notebook with the colors you use for each project and how you mixed them. This produces a nice reference library for future projects.*

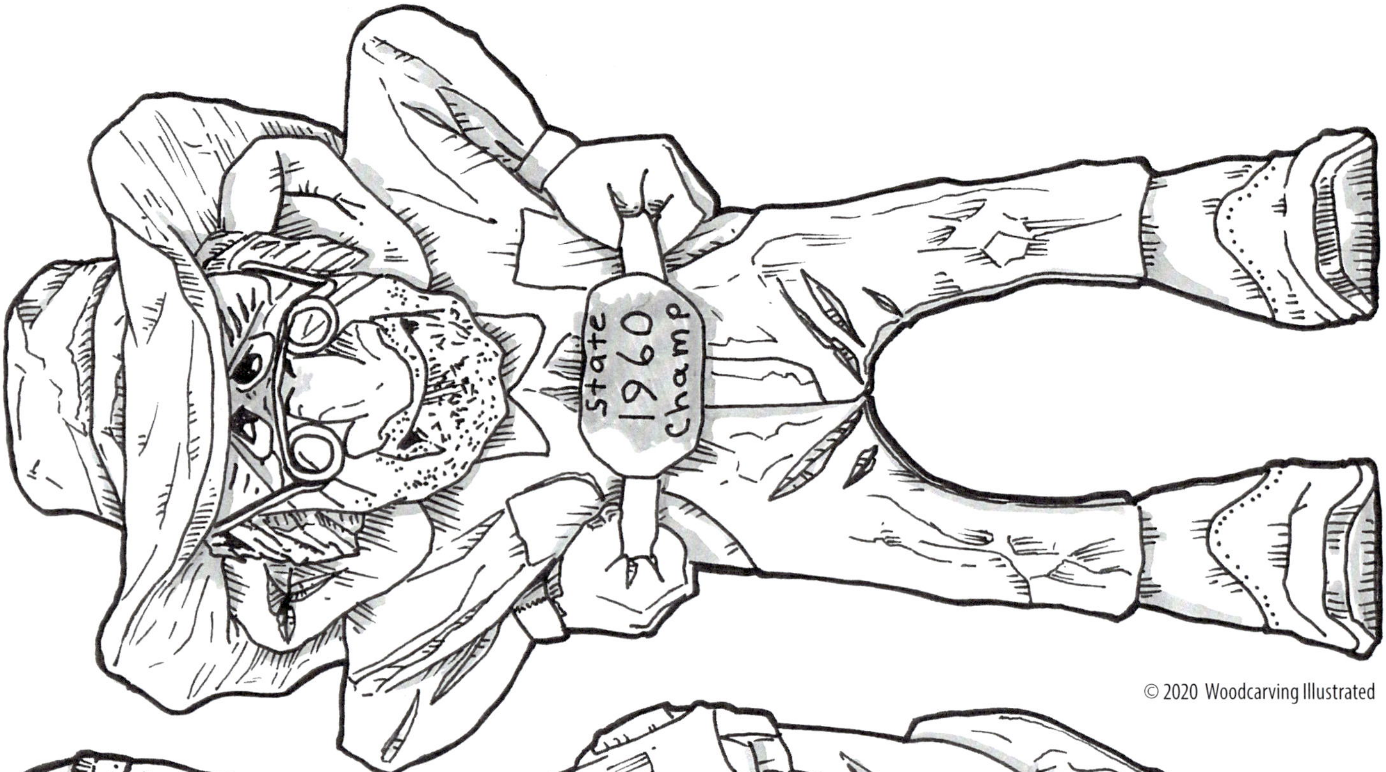

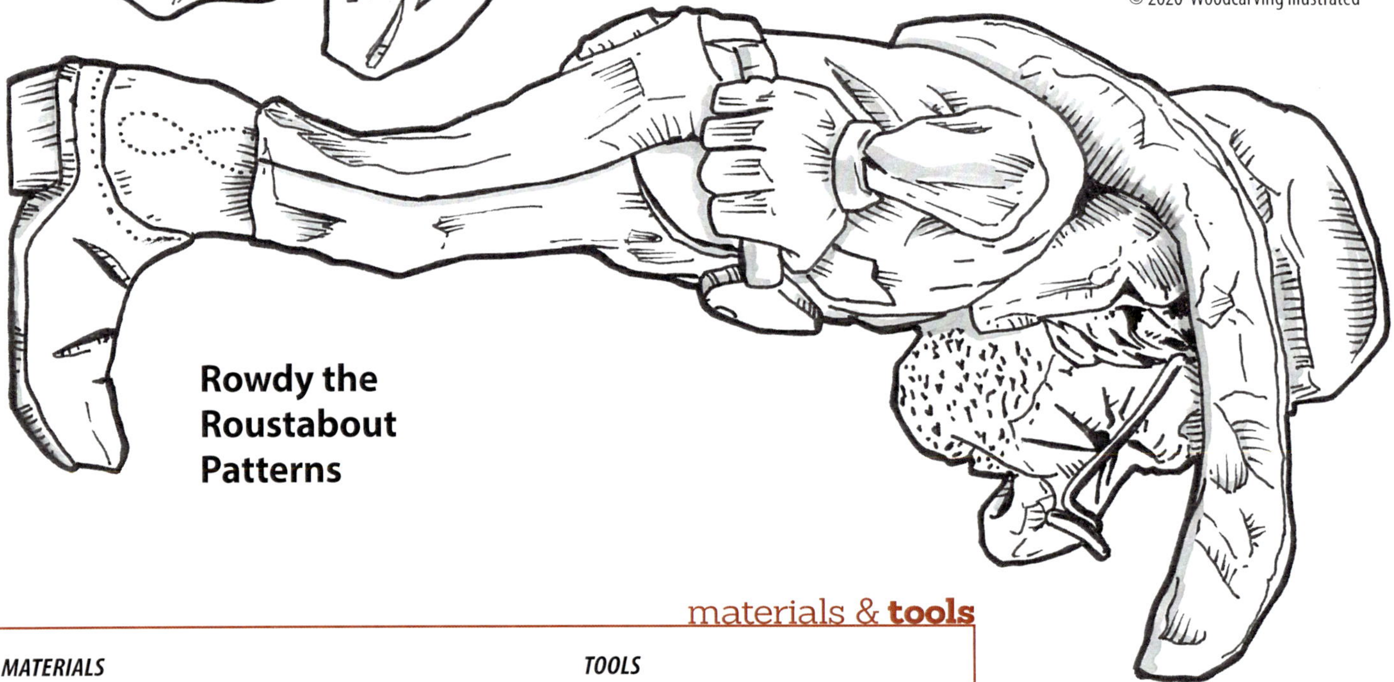

Rowdy the Roustabout Patterns

materials & **tools**

MATERIALS

- Basswood, 4" (10.2cm) square: 8" (20.3cm) long
- Pencil
- Craft wire: 12 gauge (glasses)
- Wood glue
- Dowel, 3⁄16" (5mm)-dia. (glasses)
- Cleaner and degreaser, such as Simple Green® or dish soap
- Danish oil, such as Watco natural
- Boiled linseed oil
- Soft cloth or paper towels
- Spray finish, such as Krylon® matte
- Acrylic paint, such as Delta Ceramcoat: charcoal, denim, medium flesh, mudstone, midnight blue, raw sienna; such as DecoArt Americana: napa red, raw umber, titanium white, yellow ochre; such as Craftsmart: natural beige, olive green
- Oil paint: burnt umber

The author used these products for the project. Substitute your choice of brands, tools, and materials as desired.

TOOLS

- Band saw
- Carving knife
- V-tools: 1⁄8" (3mm), 3⁄8" (10mm) 30°
- Woodburner with nibs: skew, writing
- Paintbrushes: assorted
- Denture brush
- Drill with bits: assorted small
- Sponge brush, 2 each

SPECIAL SOURCES

Roughouts for Rowdy and other projects available from Dale Green, 801-503-8754, dalegreenwoodcarving.com.

Dale Green began carving about 25 years ago. He offers weekly classes at his home studio in addition to teaching for other groups and clubs. Dale is a member of Caricature Carvers of America (CCA), and he offers a variety of roughouts on his website. Dale lives in Holladay, Utah, with his wife, Kerry, and their two dogs.

Butch the Shelf-Sitter

This bushy-browed wrangler will add charm to any book nook

By Mark Akers

Looking for friends in all the wrong places? Why not carve one that will hang around all day? This rootin'-tootin' cowboy bust can be displayed on a shelf, desk ledge, window trim, or computer monitor. I gave him simple features and eyes staring off into the distance, but don't be afraid to make this design your own.

Getting Started

Transfer the pattern views to the blank with graphite paper and a pencil. Cut the views on a band saw. Turn the blank to the front view and draw a reference line from top to bottom. Draw two more reference lines, approximately ⅛" (3mm) out from the centerline on each side. Then draw a curved reference line around the entire carving—about ½" (1.3cm) down from the top—to mark the brim of the cowboy hat.

ROUGHING OUT

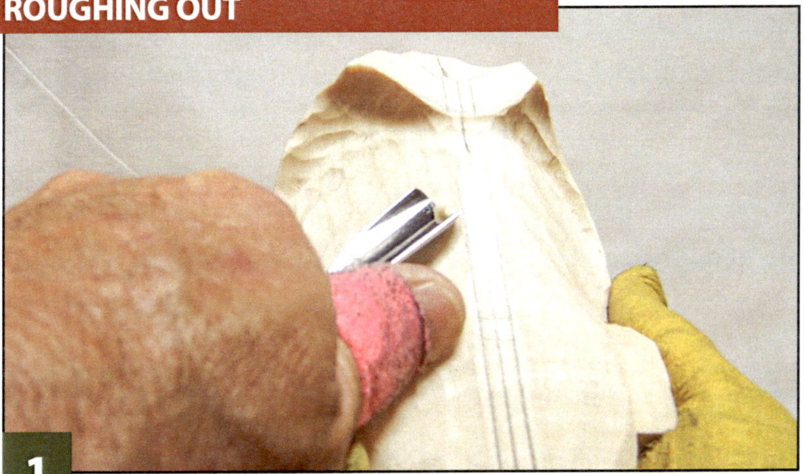

1 **Shape the face.** Using a rough out knife, taper the face on each side of the centerline up to the ½" (1.3cm) hat brim reference line, to approximately a 45° angle. Then block in the hands. Use a ⅝" (16mm) #5 gouge to taper material down and away from them. Use the gouge to carve up from the hands toward the brim of the hat, tapering the face to flow into it. Carve away material from above and below the brim so it begins to curl.

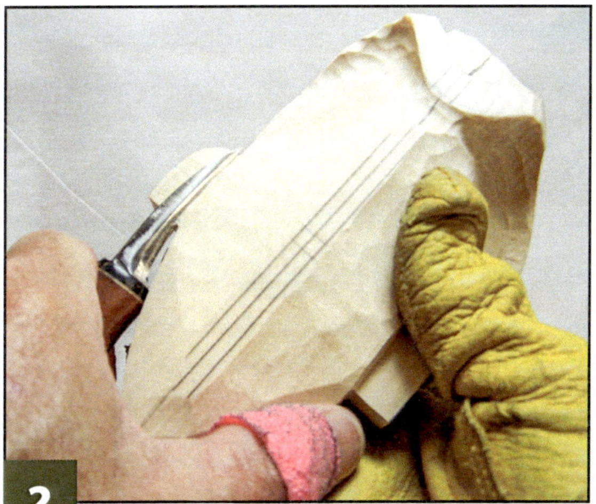

2 **Shape the hands.** Using the rough out knife, carve the hands approximately ¼" (6mm) down from face level on each side. Use the ⅝" (16mm) #5 gouge to continue shaping the hat.

3 **Locate the main features.** Use the rough out knife to create V-shaped grooves marking the middle of the eyes and the bottom of the nose. Redraw your reference lines. Then draw the sides of the face.

4 **Define the main features.** Use a 1/2" (13mm) 60° soft V-tool to carve the bridge of the nose and a channel for the eyes. Use the rough out knife to round the nose and separate it from the cheeks. Draw the mustache, sideburns, and beard. Use the knife to carve the mustache and the sideburns so they overlap the face.

5 **Carve the beard.** Use the 1/2" (13mm) 60° soft V-tool to shape and separate the beard from the face, neck, and body. Begin to separate the bandana from the beard. Then draw three fingers on each hand.

ADDING DETAILS

6 **Refine the bandana.** Use the 1/2" (13mm) 60° soft V-tool to carve folds and wrinkles in the neck scarf. *Note: Really let these lines flow. The idea is to create natural folds in the cloth. Reference the main image for a visual.* Carve a half circle just below the center of the mouth line. Carve up and into the mouth line to create a protruding bottom lip, poking out from under the mustache. Make a small, triangle-shaped chip in the center of the lip to create the mouth opening.

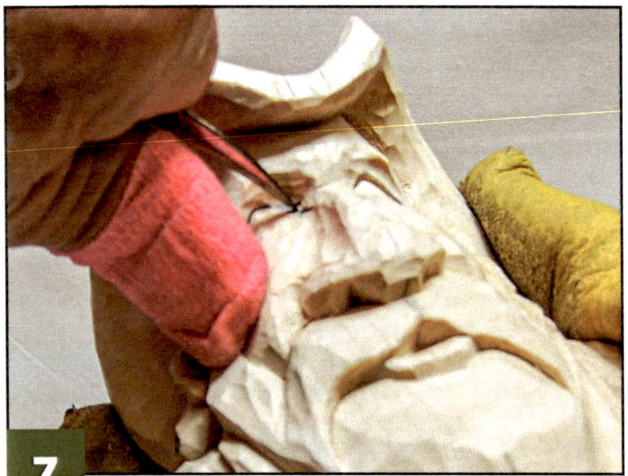

7 **Draw the eyes.** Use a detail knife to carefully carve into each eye area—making a straight line for the eyelid and a half moon shape for the lower portion. Make a small, triangular cut at the outside edge to define the eyeball and add depth.

8 **Add detail around the eyes.** Using a 1/16" (2mm) 60° V-tool, carve bags under the eyes and wrinkles into the sides of the face. *Note: Slight differences around each eye will make them look more realistic.* Use a 5/32" (4mm) 60° V-tool to carve the fingers. Then use the detail knife to add knuckle wrinkles and fingernails. Hollow out the center of the ears using the 5/8" (16mm) #5 gouge.

9 **Add hair texture.** Using a ⅛" (3mm) #11 gouge, detail the mustache, sideburns, and beard, being mindful to carve flowing—rather than straight—lines. Use a ¹⁄₁₆" (2mm) #11 gouge to go over these areas again, making new cuts. Then use the ¹⁄₁₆" (2mm) 60° V-tool to make more random cuts throughout these three sections, giving depth and interest to each area.

10 **Add eyebrows.** Use the ¹⁄₁₆" (2mm) 60° V-tool to detail the eyebrows, making lazy "S" cuts. This will give them a more filled-in, bushy look.

11 **Detail the hat.** Thin and shape the brim and top of the hat to give it character. Then inspect the carving with a critical eye. Add any final details before preparing the carving for paint.

Painting & Finishing

Working over a sink, lightly wet the carving and spray it with Simple Green® degreaser. Scrub the carving using a medium bristle brush. This process removes any marks left on the carving, as well as any oils from your hands. I paint my carvings while they are wet.

The paint mixture will vary based on the colors used. Put two to three drops of paint into one section of an ice cube tray, add two teaspoons of lukewarm water, and mix with an old paintbrush. Test your colors on a scrap of wood. *Note: I always paint the face first, and I find it beneficial to use a bright overhead light to paint by.*

Once you have finished painting, add two to three drops of burnt umber into one section of the ice cube tray. Add two teaspoons of lukewarm water and mix. Paint the thinned burnt umber over the folds, creases, and wrinkles of the bandana, and under the mustache and beard.

Antique the carving. I squeeze out 1" (2.5cm) of burnt umber oil paint per one quart of boiled linseed oil. Mix the paint and the boiled linseed oil in a 1/2-gallon can, and then dip the carving into the can. Brush the mixture onto any part of the carving you are unable to fully submerge. Set the dipped carving on clean paper towels. Wait approximately ten minutes, and then dab the carving with a clean paper towel to remove excess oils. *Note: Be sure to dab. Do not wipe the carving, as it will smear the paint.* Let the carving dry approximately 24 hours. Add finish; I used Deft clear semigloss spray. Once dry, wipe the entire carving with a crumbled up brown paper bag. Repeat this "spray and wipe" process once more.

Butch the Shelf-Sitter Patterns

Paint Notes

Bandana: black (1), titanium white (1), tomato spice (2)

Cheeks, nose, and lip: tomato spice (2)

Eyes: black (1), light cinnamon brown (1), titanium white (1)

Hair, beard, mustache, and eyebrows: burnt umber (2)

Hat: charcoal (2)

Skin: dark flesh (2), Georgia clay (2), medium flesh (2)

1 DecoArt Americana
2 Delta Ceramcoat

materials & **tools**

MATERIALS
- Basswood, 2" (5.1cm) thick: 4" x 6¼" (10.2cm x 15.9cm)
- Graphite paper
- Pencil
- Degreaser, such as Simple Green®
- Acrylic paints, such as DecoArt Americana: black, light cinnamon brown, titanium white, tomato spice; such as Delta Ceramcoat: burnt umber, charcoal, dark flesh, Georgia clay, medium flesh
- Oil paint, such as Winsor & Newton: raw umber
- Boiled linseed oil
- Paper towels
- Finish, such as Deft clear semigloss spray
- Brown paper bag

TOOLS
- Band saw
- Knives: rough out, detail
- V-tool soft: ½" (13mm) 60°
- V-tools: 1⁄16" (2mm), 5⁄32" (4mm) 60°
- #5 gouge: ⅝" (16mm),
- #11 gouge: 1⁄16" (2mm), ⅛" (3mm)
- Bristle brush: medium
- Ice cube tray (optional)
- Paintbrushes: assorted
- Plastic container

The author used these products for the project. Substitute your choice of brands, tools, and materials as desired.

Mark Akers resides in Lexington, S.C. After taking an early retirement, he now enjoys carving full-time. His love of the craft began more than 30 years ago when he attended a carving club meeting in Alton, Ill. Mark's carvings consistently win awards at competitions, including the Caricature Carvers of America's National Caricature Carvers Competition and the International Woodcarvers Congress. You can reach Mark at makers415@gmail.com.

Windy the Wrangler

Classic caricature designed to be easy to carve

By Chris Hammack

I have studied, drawn, and loved to carve old cowboys for over 35 years. I know the way an old boot wrinkles, the way a cowboy hat fits on the head, and the way a sweat stain spreads around its crown. I tried to design "Windy" to be a simple, fun project without too many fragile or difficult areas.

You can modify my design slightly to suit your preference, but first, take note of a few things. The brim of a big cowboy hat is always a problem. It is usually cross-grain and fairly fragile. Whenever possible, lay the back of the hat down against the cowboy's shoulders, avoiding the necessity of difficult cross-grain cuts. I usually shrink the torso and exaggerate the long skinny legs a little. If you make the boots bigger than normal, he will be able to stand more easily.

Getting Started

Photocopy the pattern and transfer the front and side views to the blank. Cut the rough outline of the pattern, but always leave a little extra wood at this stage. It's always easier to cut wood off than to add it back on.

ROUGHING OUT

1 **Draw the major landmarks.** Mark the arms, hands, width of the face, and crown of the hat. Don't worry about being exact; you just need to outline the main shapes at this point. Work all over the piece to keep the proportions equal.

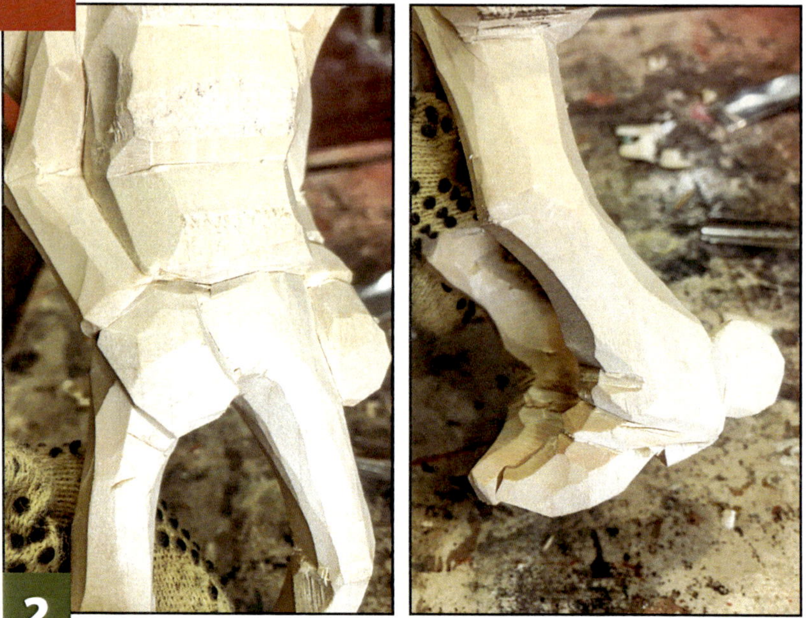

2 **Round the arms and legs.** Use a carving knife. Beginners are afraid to remove too much wood, which leaves their carving looking like a 2x4 with the edges sanded off. Don't be afraid to make some chips. Carve the outline of the vest, belt area below the stomach, and bottom of the pants. Then carve the spurs into large, round discs. *Note: Since the spurs are short grain, if they are too thin, they will break easily.* Shape the boots to a point and then carve the outline of the spur straps.

3 **Make a horizontal cut under the nose.** Use the knife. This cut establishes the length of the nose. Then use the knife to make a horizontal cut to establish the bridge of the nose. Make a cut on either side of the bridge to form rough eye sockets. The angle of these cuts determines the expression in the eyes. Angle these cuts downward to give them a haggard look. Make cuts to roughly form the mustache, beginning on either side of the nose. The mustache is big and hangs down to the cowboy's chest. Make a cut on either side to establish the sideburns and ears.

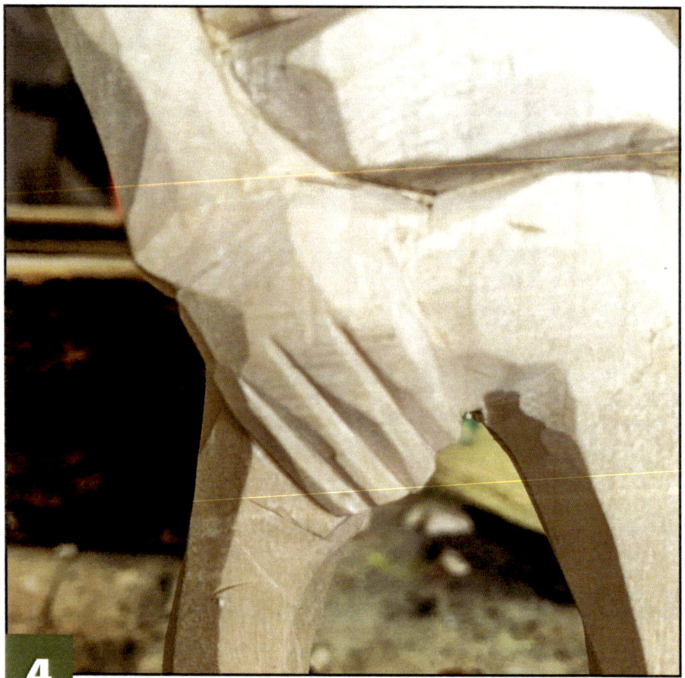

4 **Shape the hands.** The right hand is hanging in the belt by the thumb, and the left hand is holding a rifle. When roughing out, I think of the hand as a mitten: a big rectangle for the palm and fingers, and a block for the thumb. The right thumb is mostly inside the belt and not visible. The left hand has the thumb on the inside, and most of the fingers are not visible. Once the hands are roughed out, you can divide the fingers. The index and middle finger are larger than the ring and little finger. Use the knife to carve the division between the middle and ring finger first. Then carve the division between the index and ring finger and the division between the ring and little finger. Don't worry about detailing the gun hand until you carve it later.

ADDING DETAILS

5 **Make a stop cut along the top and bottom eyelids.** Use the knife. Round the eye up to the stop cuts to separate the lids from the eyeballs. Then hollow the inside of the ears with the knife.

6 **Carve the hair and mustache detail.** Use a ⅛" (3mm) 60° V-tool. Use the knife to break up the ends of the hair to look a little more natural. Make stabbing cuts with the V-tool to simulate beard stubble. Finish carving the hat. Thin the edges of the brim, but leave it thicker where it joins the crown for additional strength.

7 **Carve the wrinkles into the shirt and pants.** Use the knife. Add more wrinkles at the elbows and knees. Then add a few wrinkles where the shirt tucks into the pants. *Note: Don't overdo the wrinkles; sometimes less is more.* Use the knife to carve the vest buttons and the belt buckle. Add the pocket details to the back and sides of the jeans with the ⅛" (3mm) 60° V-tool. Use the same tool to add the heel and sole details and the spur strap. Carefully carve the details onto the rowels (points) of the spurs.

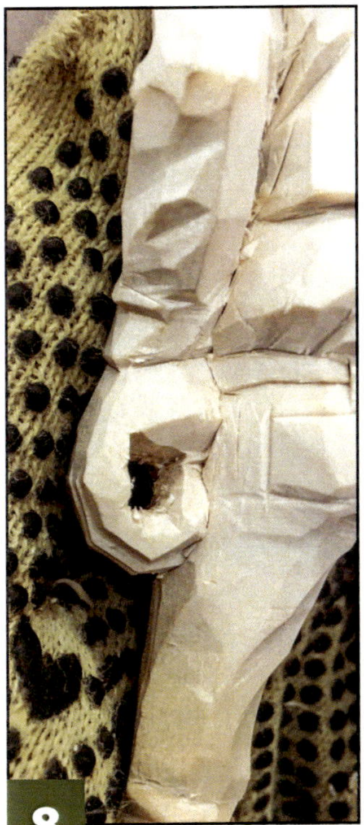

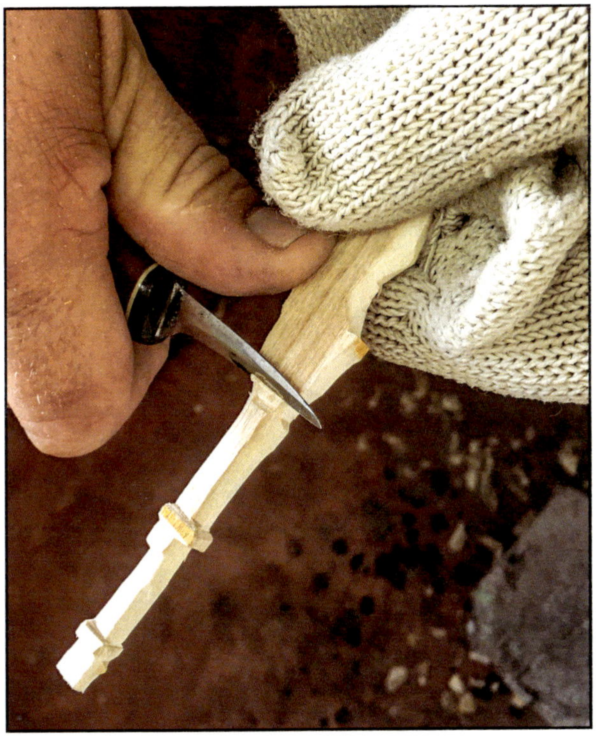

8 **Carve the gun to fit into his hand.** Use the knife. Then twist a micro gouge like a drill bit to bore a hole halfway through the hand. Twist the gouge up from the bottom to meet in the middle. Enlarge the hole with the knife to fit the rifle. After you've carved the rifle, carve the finger details. Go back over the carving and clean up any fuzzy areas. Double-check your work.

Painting and Finishing

I use acrylic paints thinned with water so the grain of the wood shows through. When in doubt, make the paint thinner. You can always add another coat to darken it if you like, but removing paint is difficult.

Once dry, seal the carving with several coats of spray lacquer. Then apply Minwax aged oak gel stain, thinned slightly with mineral spirits, to the carving and immediately wipe it off. Allow some of the stain to remain in the wrinkles and other low spots, but make sure you get it off the high spots. If the stain doesn't wipe off, remove it using a rag dampened with mineral spirits.

Windy the Wrangler Patterns

Paint Notes

Iris: black (1)

Eye highlight: white (1)

Skin: medium flesh (1)

Boots, belt, vest, hat: black (1)

Spurs, belt buckle: silver (1)

Spur straps: brown (1)

Hair, beard: white (1)

Facial tinting: cadmium red light (2)

Rifle barrel: black (1)

Rifle stock: brown (1)

Buttons: undiluted black (1)

1 Delta Ceramcoat
2 Liquitex

materials & **tools**

MATERIALS

- Basswood, 3" (7.6cm) square: cowboy, 7½" (19.1cm) long
- Basswood, ½" (1.3cm) thick: gun, 1" x 4" (2.5cm x 10.2cm)
- Acrylic paint: such as Delta Ceramcoat: black, brown, medium flesh, silver, white: such as Liquitex: cadmium red light, silver, white
- Lacquer: spray
- Gel stain, such as Minwax: aged oak
- Mineral spirits
- Rag (optional)

TOOLS

- Carving knife
- V-tool: ⅛" (3mm) 60°
- Micro gouge: 1⁄16" (2mm) or ⅛" (3mm)

The author used these products for the project. Substitute your choice of brands, tools, and materials as desired.

Chris Hammack, a member of the Caricature Carvers of America, has moved to Mexico but returns to the United States to teach classes. For more of Chris's work or to see a class schedule, visit his website (chrishammackart.com), call him at 254-485-0668, or e-mail him at chris@chrishammack.com.

Hank the Rooster

Curved cuts and easy-carve joints bring this comical character to life

By Jim Feather

I've always enjoyed old-fashioned jointed carvings. I played around with the idea of a rooster cowboy for a while, and then decided to make him move. This is a great project for beginners because if you mess up one area, it's simple to carve a new one to fit.

I've found that my carvings turn out best when I rough out the entire carving first. Many carvers start carving the details way too early. Rough it out first, and then carve the details.

Getting Started

Start by transferring the outline of the rooster to the blank and cutting the outline with a band saw. Draw a centerline onto the blank, and then draw the other major landmarks, such as the leg sockets.

ROUGHING OUT

1 **Rough out the main body piece.** Use a knife or a ¾" (19mm) #3 gouge to taper the top of the head from the cheeks toward the comb. Use the knife to taper the tail from the bulging middle area to the top. Remove as much wood as possible from the leg slots with a ¼" (6mm) #11 gouge and clean up the slots with a knife.

2 **Draw the jaw and wattle.** Use the ¾" (19mm) #3 gouge to make a stop cut along the bottom of the wattle and to taper the neck up to it. Refine the wattle and the back of the neck with the knife. Leave extra wood around the neck for the bandana. Make the wattle match on both sides of the face.

3 **Rough out the front of the wattle.** Round the breast up to the wattle using the knife. Draw the underside of the wattle. Use a knife to make a stop cut along the inside of the wattle and relieve up to it, clearing a triangular section under the wattle. Draw the bottoms of the cheeks. Use a knife to remove some of the excess wood on the sides of the beak.

4 **Rough-shape the head.** With the ¾" (19mm) #3 gouge, round the top of the head up to the comb. Use a knife to make a stop cut where the head and comb meet and relieve up to it, separating the comb from the head. Make a stop cut along the cheek, and use the same gouge to give the wattle a swooping shape as you relieve up to the stop cut. Round the cheeks into the stop cut.

5 **Shape the vest and bandana.** Draw the bandana. Then use a knife to make a long sweeping stop cut along the line and relieve up to it. Make stop cuts along the edges of the vest and relieve up to them to separate the vest from the breast. Use the same technique to separate the vest from the back. Remove the saw marks from the vest. Use the ¼" (6mm) #11 gouge to separate the bandana knot from the back.

ADDING DETAILS

6 **Refine the vest and back.** Use the knife to round the tail and create a bulging feather group near the top. Mark the base of the tail and the shoulders. Make a stop cut at the tail base and relieve up to it to separate the tail from the hips, and then refine the hips. Use a 1⁄16" (2mm) #11 veiner to separate the vest from the tail. Use the 3⁄4" (19mm) #3 gouge to lower the vest around the shoulders. Make a stop cut around the center bulge of the knot with a knife and relieve up to it. Leave the knot oversized; you will add the details later.

7 **Carve the face.** From the front, the beak is triangular. Taper the top of the beak upward with a knife. Round the tip and bottom slightly. Remove the sharp corners near the eye sockets. Carve the brow bone using the 1⁄16" (2mm) #11 veiner. Use the knife to refine the intersections between the beak and face and the cheeks and wattle, to separate the comb from the forehead, and to create an eyebrow ridge.

8 **Carve the eyes.** Make dots in the corners of the eyes. Draw the top and bottom of each eye. Use the knife to stab along both lines at the inside corner of one eye, extending the cuts halfway across the eye. Relieve up to the cuts and remove a triangular chip of wood. Use the same technique on the outside corner. Round the eyeball up to the top line and down to the bottom line. Then round the eyeball between the corners. Repeat for the second eye.

9 **Refine the comb.** Use the 3⁄4" (19mm) #3 gouge to round the top of one side of the comb so it appears to bend to the side. Use the knife to make a stop cut along the bottom of the comb on the opposite side. With the gouge, undercut the comb down to the stop cut, matching the profile carved on the other side. Use the knife to carve above the eyebrow to separate the brow from the head.

10 **Refine the beak.** It appears that the beak is sharply hooked, but that's an illusion. Shape the underside of the beak with the knife and remove the bottom corners. To give the beak a hooked shape, use the 3⁄4" (19mm) #3 gouge to carve a slight curve along the underside of the beak toward the rooster's head.

11 **Carve the tail feathers.** Draw the feather groups. Carve along the lines with a 3⁄16" (5mm) 45° V-tool. Start with the top feather group and work your way down. Use the knife to make deep stop cuts in the V-grooves. Round the feathers into the stop cuts. Deepen the cuts to imply that some feather groups sit on top of other feather groups.

12 **Refine the wattle and beak.** Use the ¾" (19mm) #3 gouge to carve a greater curve into the wattle so it flares dramatically at the bottom. Curve the wattle up to the bottom of the cheeks. Draw the mouth opening and stop cut along the line with the knife. Relieve up to the stop cut from below so the bottom jaw fits under the rest of the beak.

13 **Finish the bandana.** Shape the knot and ends using the knife. Use the 3⁄16" (5mm) 45° V-tool to carve an asterisk making the folds on the knot. Use a 3⁄16" (5mm) #9 gouge to carve wrinkles from the knot to the front. Use the 1⁄16" (2mm) #11 micro veiner to deepen the wrinkles and create shadows. Use the knife to undercut the bandana so it sits on top of the vest. Undercut the knot using the micro veiner.

14 **Finish the shoulders and vest.** Draw the oval shoulder. Make a stop cut on the line using the knife. Relieve to the stop cut from the inside to make a shallow groove around the shoulder. Draw the vest pocket and carve along the lines with the 1⁄16" (2mm) #11 micro veiner. Relieve around the pocket with the knife so the pocket protrudes slightly. Use a pounce wheel, awl, or nail set to create stitching marks in the edge of the vest.

CARVING THE ATTACHMENTS

15 **Shape the legs and boots.** Use the knife to trim the bottom of the thighs so the rooster sits flat. Carefully remove wood from the tabs until they move freely in the slots. Round the thighs and boots. Cutting from the toe toward the leg, carve the up-pointing toe on top of the boot. Remove wood from under the toe to match the profile. Draw the sole and make a stop cut along the line. Carve down to the stop cut to separate the sole. Draw the heel, and remove a triangular chip of wood to separate the heel from the bottom of the boot.

16 **Finish the boots and legs.** Draw the top of the boot and make a stop cut along the line with a knife. Carve down to the stop cut, and undercut the edges of the boot top to separate it from the leg. Taper the boot from the top so it flares slightly. Then position the thigh and boot pieces together and mark the joint holes. Using a ⅛" (3mm) drill bit, drill through the hip and thigh tab on each side. Then drill from the inside of the thigh slot, through the boot tab, and partway through the outside thigh slot. Do not drill all the way through the outside edge of the slot.

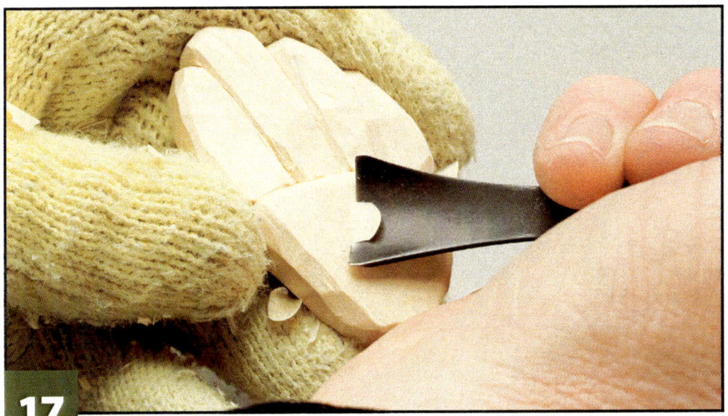

17 **Carve the wings.** Remove the saw marks from the edges of the wings. Then remove the sharp corners. Sketch the feathers. Make a stop cut along the lines and carve up to the lines to separate the feathers. Use the ¾" (19mm) #3 gouge to remove the saw marks from the back of the wings. Make sure that no surface remains uncarved.

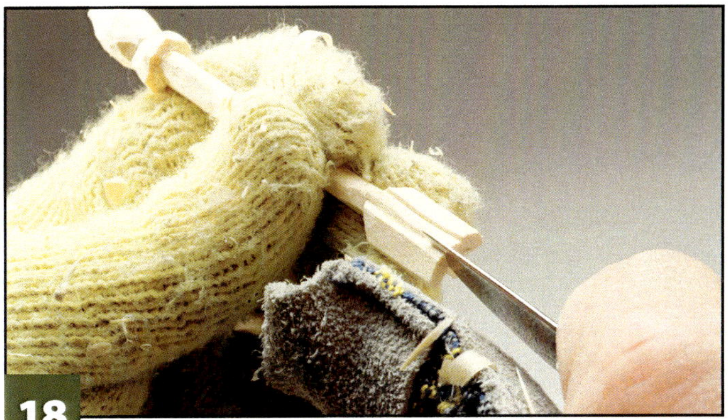

18 **Carve the arrow.** I carve the entire arrow as one piece and cut it in half to insert it into the hat. Use the knife to remove the sharp corners and round the shaft. Carve the feathers on one end and the arrowhead on the other. Use the tip of the knife to carve the feather details. Carve lines in the feathers with the 1⁄16" (2mm) #11 micro veiner.

19 **Carve the inside of the hat.** Scoop out the inside of the hat using a 5⁄16" (8mm) #11 and a ½" (13mm) #7 bent gouge until it fits on the head. Shape the crown with the knife. Make a stop cut along the brim and carve up to it to separate the crown from the brim. Carve from the brim up to the crown with the knife and bent gouge. Switch back and forth between these tools to remove the sharp corners and saw marks from the bottom and crown, separate the brim from the crown, shape the crown, and carve the upturned brim.

20 **Finish carving the hat.** Use the ¼" (6mm) #11 gouge to refine the edges of the brim. Leave the brim thick until you carve the curl. Use the knife to thin the edges. Then use the knife to cut an angled groove at the bottom of the gouge cut. Carve the outside of the brim and the creases; the creases are subtle, but they contribute to the overall look of the carving. Cut the arrow in half. Choose a drill bit slightly smaller than the diameter of the arrow shaft and drill a hole through the hat. Ream out the hole with a larger bit if necessary. Dry-fit the arrow into the hole in the hat.

PAINTING & FINISHING

I use thinned artist acrylic paints for this project, such as JoSonja or Liquitex. Artist paints have more pigment than craft paints, and a tube of artist acrylic will last a long time. Unless otherwise specified, I thin 1 part paint with 3 parts water (1:3).

Washes of acrylic paint can make raw wood blotchy. I seal the carving with Watco Danish oil fruitwood stain, which gives the wood a nice color, minimizes blotchiness, and prevents raw wood from showing in the deep crevices. Apply a coat of Danish oil to the entire carving with a cheap acid brush, allow it to sit for 5 minutes, and dab off the excess oil with a paper towel. Allow the oil to cure overnight before you start painting.

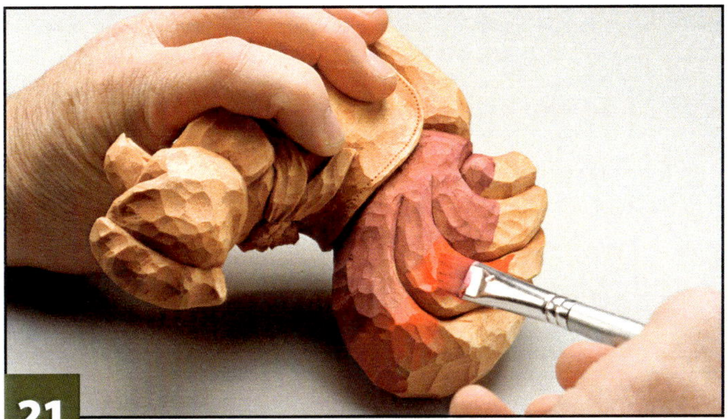

21 **Paint the tail.** Mix burgundy, purple, and water in a 1:1:3 ratio to create reddish-purple. Apply the mixture to the base of the tail feathers, ending at a different place on each feather. Mix napthol crimson with water (1:3) and paint the next section of the feathers, blending the crimson with the edges of the wet reddish-purple. Paint the wing feathers using the same method.

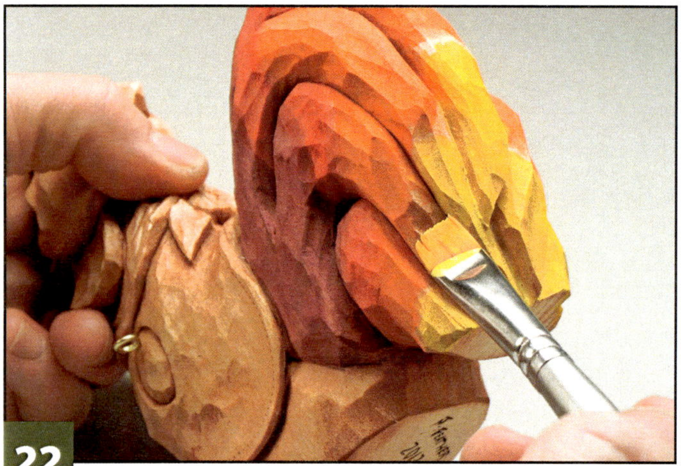

22

Finish painting the feathers and the beak. Thin vermilion with water and paint the middle section of the tail feathers. Paint this wash over the previously painted colors to blend and brighten them. Use the same technique to paint the wing feathers. Thin cadmium yellow medium with water and paint the tips of the feathers. Pull this light color over the other colors to blend them. Repeat on the wing feathers. Paint the beak with the cadmium yellow medium as well.

23

Paint the other major elements. Paint the comb and wattle with thinned napthol crimson. Paint the body, head, and legs with the reddish-purple mix. Remember the areas where you can see the shoulder and underarm through the vest. Paint the bandana with thinned aqua. Paint the feathers on the arrow with thinned napthol crimson and the point on the arrow with thinned carbon black. Leave the hat, vest, and boots unpainted. Glue the pieces of the arrow into the holes in the hat.

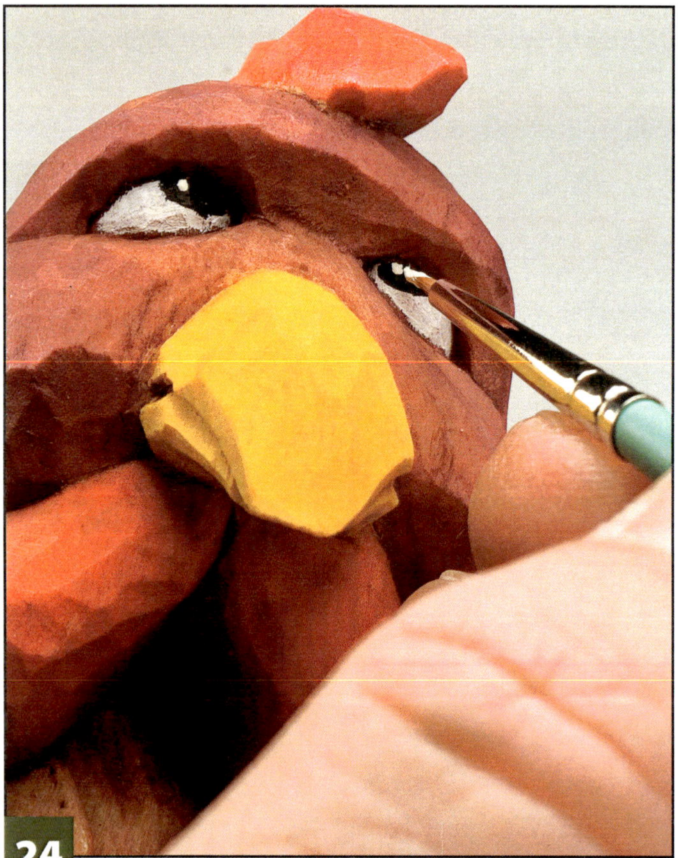

24

Finish painting. Thin warm white slightly and paint the eyes; allow the paint to dry. Thin carbon black slightly and paint the pupils positioned so the rooster is looking up at the arrow through his hat. Use the thinned warm white and carbon black to paint the pattern of two white dots and one black dot on the bandana. Add a spot of white to the pupil for the eye glint. Pick up undiluted purple, wipe most of it off the brush, and drybrush the tail and wing feathers to give them a subtle shine and highlight the tool marks.

25

Assemble the carving. Coat three ⅛" (3mm) dowels in Danish oil. One dowel (approximately 2" [5.1cm] long) goes through the hips and one dowel (approximately 1" [2.5cm] long) goes through each thigh/knee joint. Place the boot in position and thread a dowel through the leg slot almost into position. Use a toothpick to add a dot of glue to the dowel at the surface of the leg, and push the dowel into place. Make sure to keep the glue away from the inner part of each joint, as this will restrict the moving parts' ability to swing. Trim the dowel flush with the surface of the leg. Use the same technique to attach the leg to the hip. Use two small eye screws on each side to attach the wings to the body. Hang the wings with the longer feathers toward the front. Seal the carving with two or three coats of Deft satin clear wood finish. Place the hat on the rooster's head.

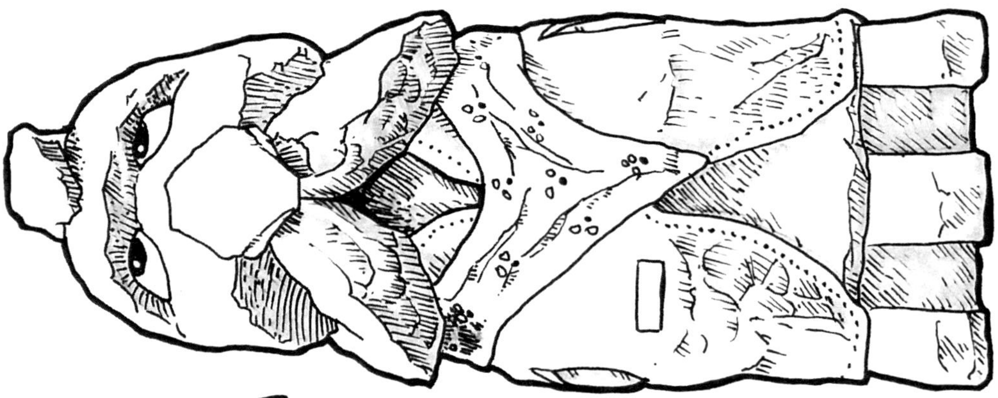

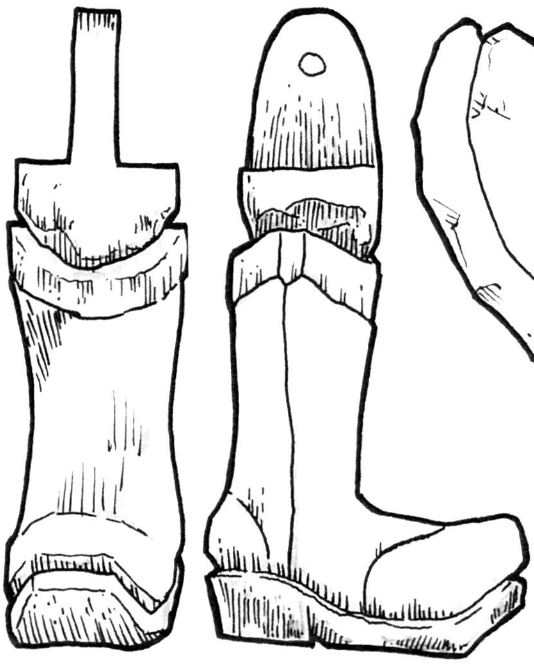

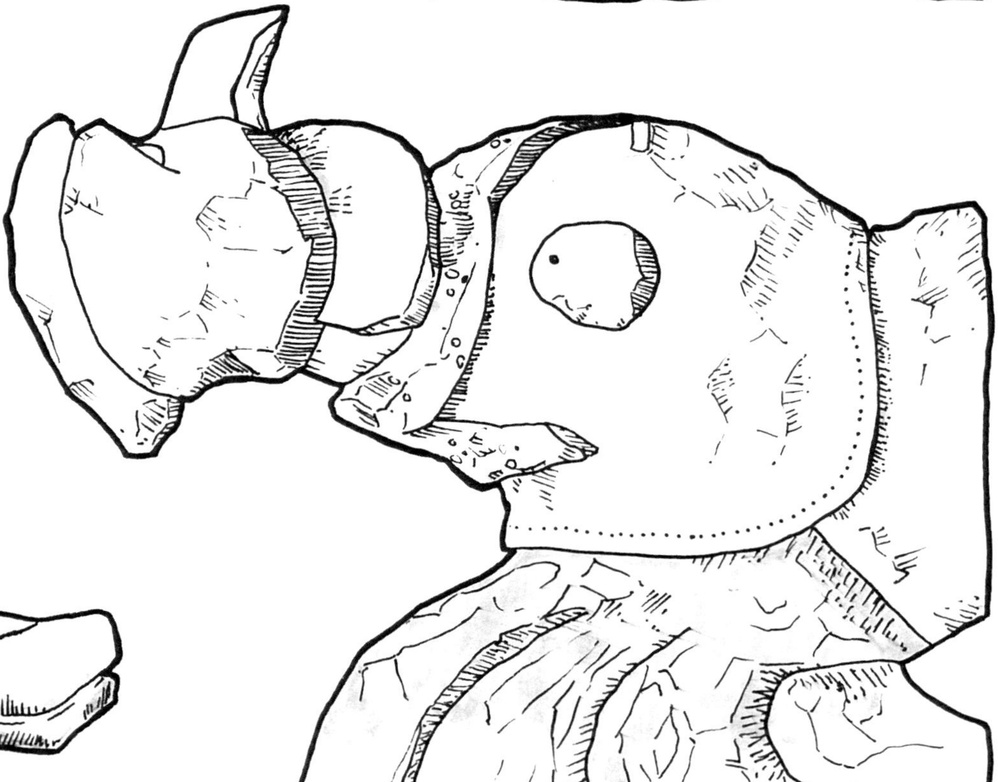

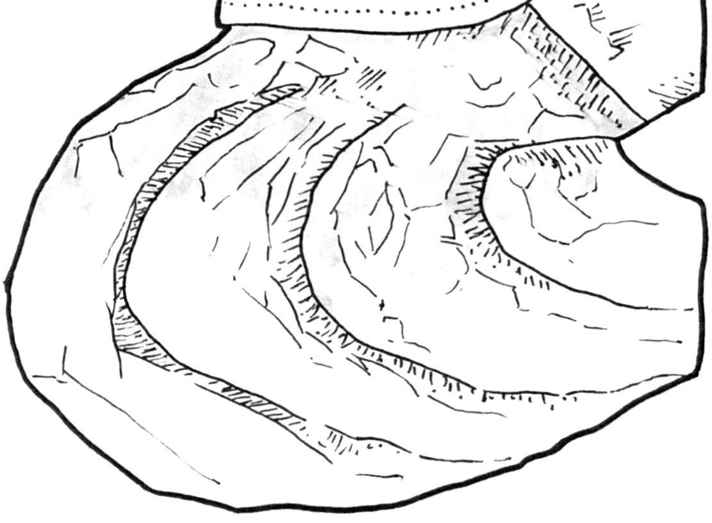

Hank the Rooster Patterns

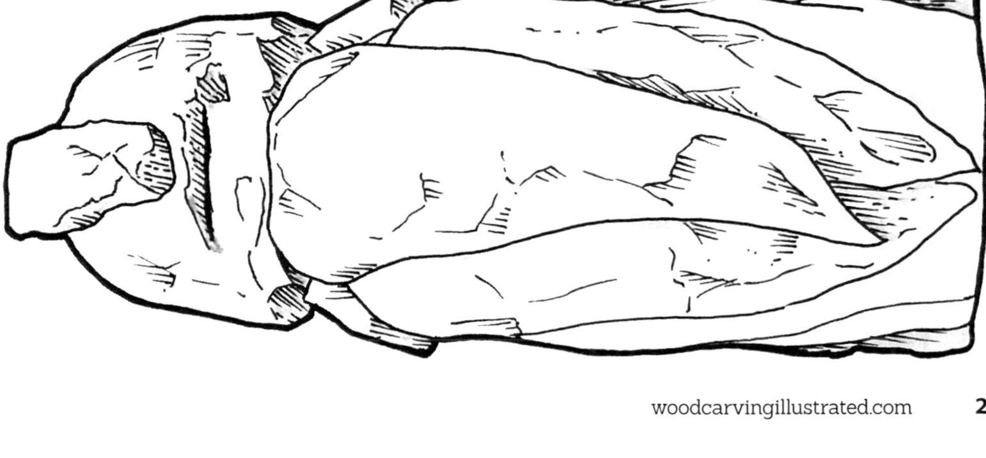

Hank the Rooster Patterns

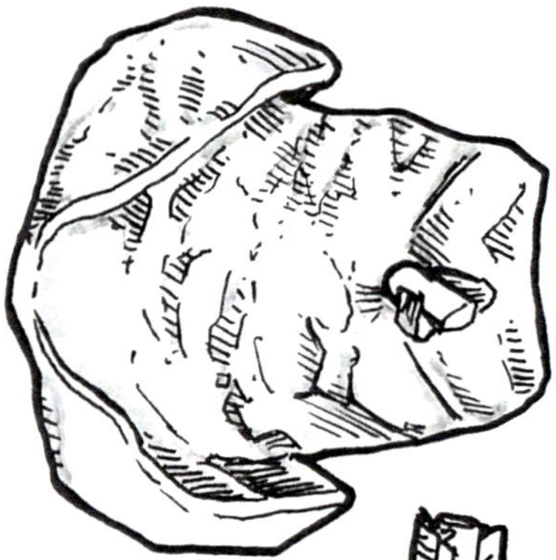

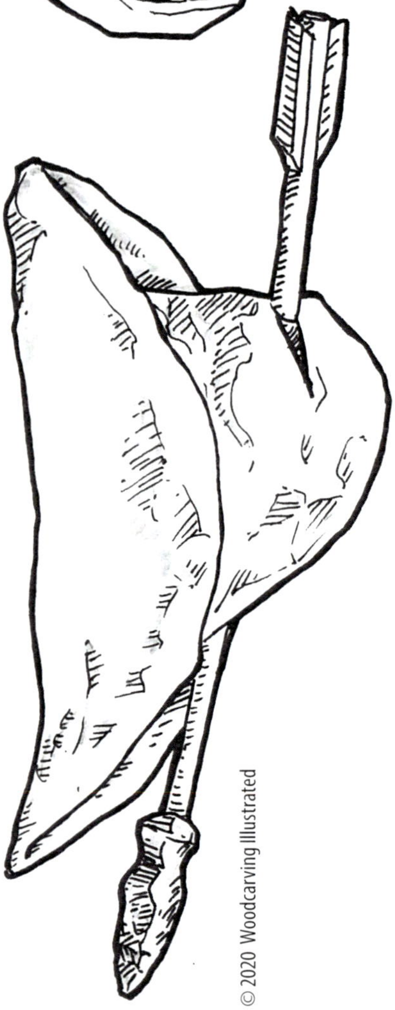

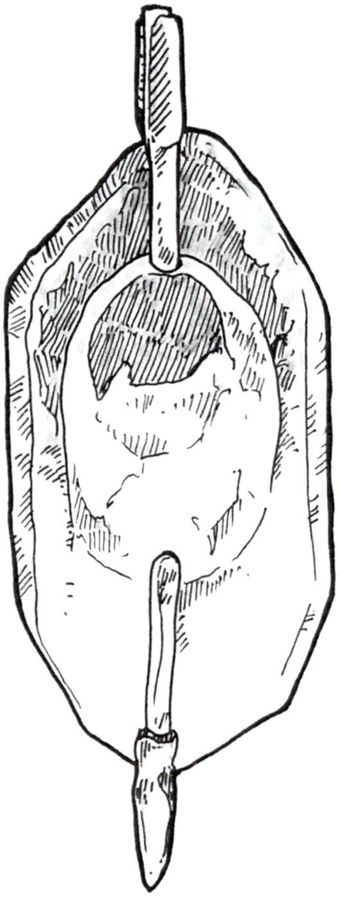

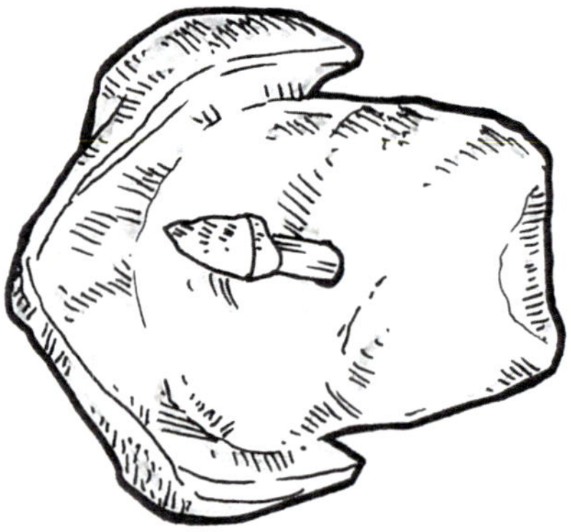

MATERIALS

- Basswood, 2" (5.1cm) thick: body, 5¼" x 5½" (13.3cm x 14cm); hat, 2" x 4" (5.1cm x 10.2cm)
- Basswood, ¾" (1.9cm) thick: upper legs, 2 each ¾" x 2½" (1.9cm x 6.4cm); lower legs, 2 each 2" x 3½" (5.1cm x 8.9cm)
- Basswood, ⅜" (1cm) thick: wings, 2 each 1½" x 2¾" (3.8cm x 7cm); arrow, ⅜" x 6" (1cm x 15.2cm)
- Danish oil, such as Watco fruitwood stain
- Artist acrylic paints, such as JoSonja or Liquitex: aqua, burgundy, cadmium yellow medium, carbon black, napthol crimson, purple, vermilion, warm white
- Dowel, ⅛" (3mm)-dia: 3 each 8" (20.3cm) long
- Wood glue
- Paper towels
- Toothpicks
- Brass screw eyes: 4 each 3⁄16" (5mm)-dia.
- Spray finish, such as Deft: clear satin

TOOLS

- Carving knife
- #3 gouge: ¾" (19mm)
- #9 gouge: 3⁄16" (5mm)
- #11 gouges: ¼" (6mm), 5⁄16" (8mm)
- #7 gouge: ½" (13mm) bent
- Micro tool: 1⁄16" (2mm) #11 gouge (veiner)
- V-tool: 3⁄16" (5mm) 45°
- Awl, nail set, or pounce wheel
- Paintbrushes: assorted
- Acid brush
- Pliers
- Drill with bit: ⅛" (3mm)-dia.

The author used these products for the project. Substitute your choice of brands, tools, and materials as desired.

Jim Feather lives in Landisville, Pa., with his wife, Gloria. A woodworker and caricature carver for many years, he teaches an adult carving class and demonstrates the art at the local elementary school during its annual Pennsylvania Heritage Day event. View more of Jim's work at facebook.com/jimfeatherwoodcarver.

Straight-Shot Stoney

Bold cuts are the secret to this rustic design

By Chris Hammack

I've carved bottle stoppers for more than 25 years, and they are still my favorite projects because they're a wonderful way to practice facial expressions.

Getting Started

Transfer the front and side view patterns to the blank. Use a band saw to cut the outline. Draw a centerline on the front and add the major landmarks, such as the hat brim, eyes, nose, and ears. Remove some of the excess wood around these major landmarks.

I carve primarily with a knife, and prefer one with a large blade, such as a 4" (10.2cm)-long Helvie. This helps achieve bold, rough cuts. The only other tools you need for this carving are a good size gouge for inside the brim of the hat and a small V-tool for the hair and beard detail.

Painting and Finishing

I use acrylic paint thinned with water to a wash consistency. I use a medium flesh color for the skin. Drybrush the beard so it doesn't completely cover the skin color below it. Drybrush cadmium red onto the tip of the nose, around the eyes, and on the outside of the ears.

For the antiquing process, I use one-step dark walnut stain + polyurethane diluted with mineral spirits. Dip the piece in the mixture or brush it onto the piece and let it sit for a couple of minutes. Then wipe off the excess. I leave the dark mixture in the cracks and crevices in the eyes and in the beard.

The final step is to carefully drill a 5/16" (8mm)-diameter by ¾" (1.9cm)-deep hole into the bottom of the neck and a 5/16" (8mm)-diameter by ½" (1.3cm)-deep hole into a #8 cork. Glue a 5/16" (8mm)-diameter by 1¼" (3.2cm)-long dowel into the neck and glue the cork onto the dowel.

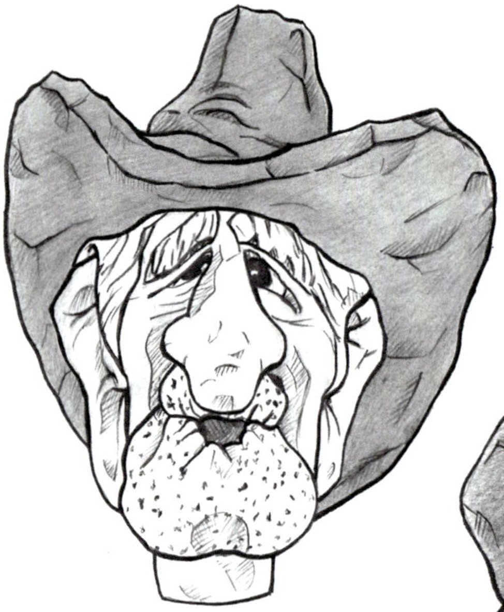

Straight-Shot Stoney Patterns

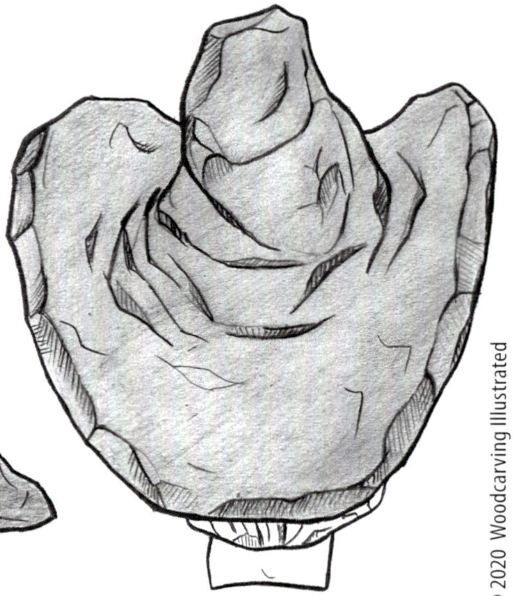

materials & **tools**

MATERIALS

- Basswood: 2¾" (7cm) square: 3¼" (8.3cm) long
- Cork, #8
- Dowel, 5⁄16" (8mm)-dia.
- Acrylic paint: such as Delta Ceramcoat: black, medium flesh; such as Liquitex: cadmium red; and colors of choice for eyes, beard, and hair
- Finish, such as Rust-Oleum one-step stain + polyurethane: dark walnut
- Mineral spirits

TOOLS

- Band saw
- Carving knife
- Gouge of choice
- V-tool: small
- Drill with bit: 5⁄16" (8mm)-dia.
- Paintbrushes: assorted

The author used these products for the project. Substitute your choice of brands, tools, and materials as desired.

Chris Hammack, a member of the Caricature Carvers of America, has moved to Mexico but returns to the United States to teach classes. For more of Chris's work or to see a class schedule, visit his website (chrishammackart.com), call him at 254-485-0668, or e-mail him at chris@chrishammack.com.

Sheriff Santa

Visit the Wild West in style with this classic holiday icon

By Gerald and Barb Sears

Woodburning and painting add the details that give this cowboy Santa a lot of down-home charm. I use both an metal engraver and a woodburner. The engraver does an excellent job creating texture on the trim of the coat and hat. The woodburner is great for little details.

Getting Started

Transfer the patterns to the blank using your preferred method. Cut the outline with a band saw. Draw a centerline on the front and add the major landmarks, such as the hat brim, beard, hands, legs, and boots. Remove some of the excess wood around these major landmarks.

Adding Details

Carve Santa using the tools and techniques of your choice. To make the paint application easier, try to keep the carving clean from dirt and oil.

Woodburn the trees on the boots, the holly leaves on the belt buckle, and all of the main cuts on the carving; the seams, the creases in the clothing, the boots, around the eyeballs, and the eyelids. Use a low-heat setting so that these lines are light.

Painting and Finishing

After adding the details, prepare the carving for paint. Reference the Paint Notes on page 32.

Once the paint is dry, apply a coat of a 50-50 mixture of boiled linseed oil and paint thinner. Once dry, spray lightly with Deft semigloss finish. Add a piece of felt to the bottom of the base, if desired.

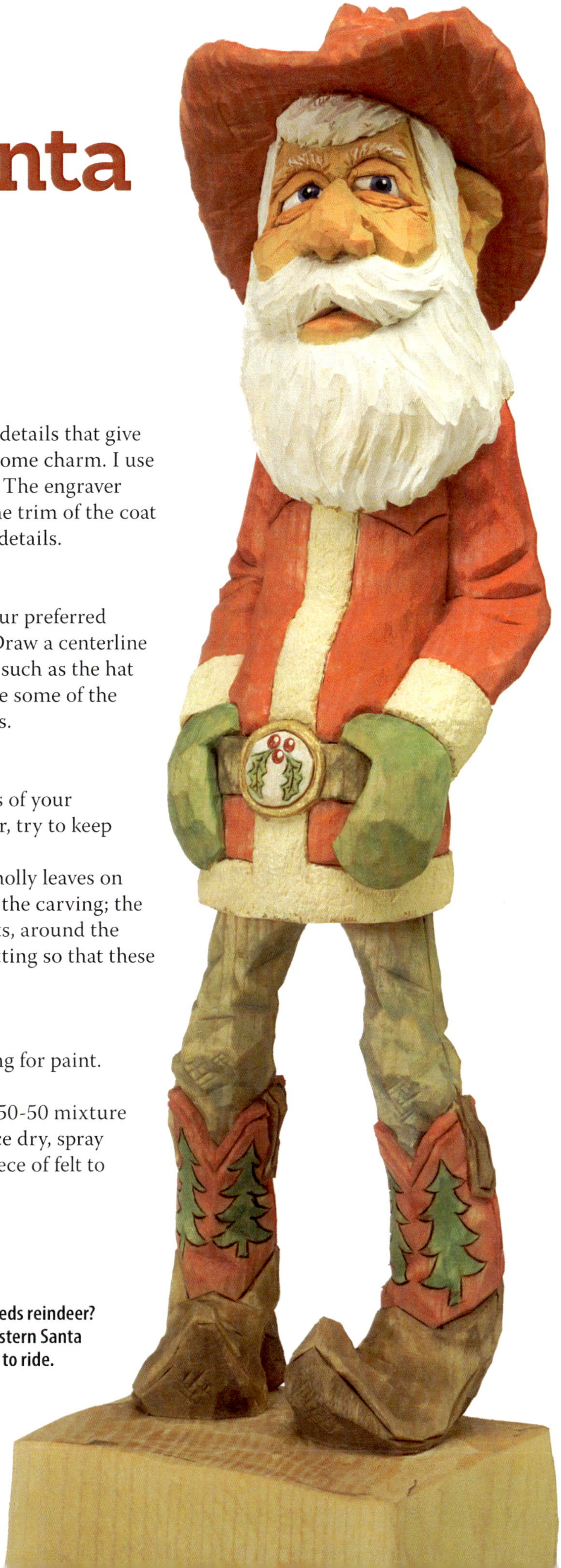

Who needs reindeer? This Western Santa is ready to ride.

Sheriff Santa Patterns

Paint Notes

Coat, hat, boot tops: 2 drops Santa red (1) in 1 tbsp of water

Gloves, trees on boots, holly leaves: 2 drops of Christmas green (2) in 1 tbsp of water

Boots: 2 drops of burnt umber (2) in 1 tbsp of water

Belt, pants: 2 drops black (2) in 1 tbsp of water

Coat, hat trim: ivory (2) with just enough water to make it spread

Beard, eyes: white (2) with just enough water to make it spread

Berries on buckle: Santa red (1) with white (2) highlights

Flesh color: medium flesh (2)

Blush on cheeks: cadmium red light (2) mixed with medium flesh (2)

Eyes: white (2) with denim blue (2) for iris, black (2) dot for pupil, and tiny white (2) dot for highlight

1 DecoArt Americana
2 Delta Ceramcoat

materials & **tools**

MATERIALS

- Basswood: 3" (7.6cm) square, 11" (27.9cm) long
- Acrylic paints: such as DecoArt Americana: Santa red; such as Delta Ceramcoat: black, burnt umber, cadmium red light, Christmas green, denim blue, ivory, medium flesh, white
- Boiled linseed oil
- Paint thinner
- Finish, such as Deft semigloss
- Toothpick
- Felt (optional)

TOOLS

- Band saw
- Carving knife
- Gouges: assorted
- Engraver
- Woodburner with nibs: assorted
- Paintbrushes: assorted

The author used these products for the project. Substitute your choice of brands, tools, and materials as desired.

Gerald Sears and his wife, Barb, live on 20 acres in the Ozarks of the Southwest Missouri. The Sears have been carving and painting together for over 55 years. Gerald is a self-taught woodcarver and an original member of the Caricature Carvers of America. Barb, also self-taught, uses paints to breathe life into his characters. See more of their work at gnbsearswoodcarving.com.

Snowman Clint

Woodburned lines and painting tips help you bring Frosty to the Midwest

By Gerald and Barb Sears

On page 31, I presented my cowboy version of Santa. Now I have given a traditional snowman a similar treatment. For this snowman, the hat is key—you've got to keep the sun off his face!

Carving the Snowman

For roughing out, I use a large gouge (1" to 1½" [25mm to 38mm] wide) with a mallet. *Note: Always clamp your project in a vise when using a mallet and gouge. It's easier to stand up when you're removing a lot of wood.* After roughing out, I move down to hand and palm tools, as well as a long thin-bladed knife to add the details.

When you have finished carving, use a woodburner to lightly burn (at a low heat setting) along the clothing seams and the lines between the clothes and the body. I also burned the holly leaves on the coat. (Practice your burning technique on scrap wood beforehand.) Then buff the piece with a Scotch-Brite® pad in a rotary tool to blend the woodburned areas and knock off the edges of the tool marks, softening the overall look of the piece.

Paint Notes

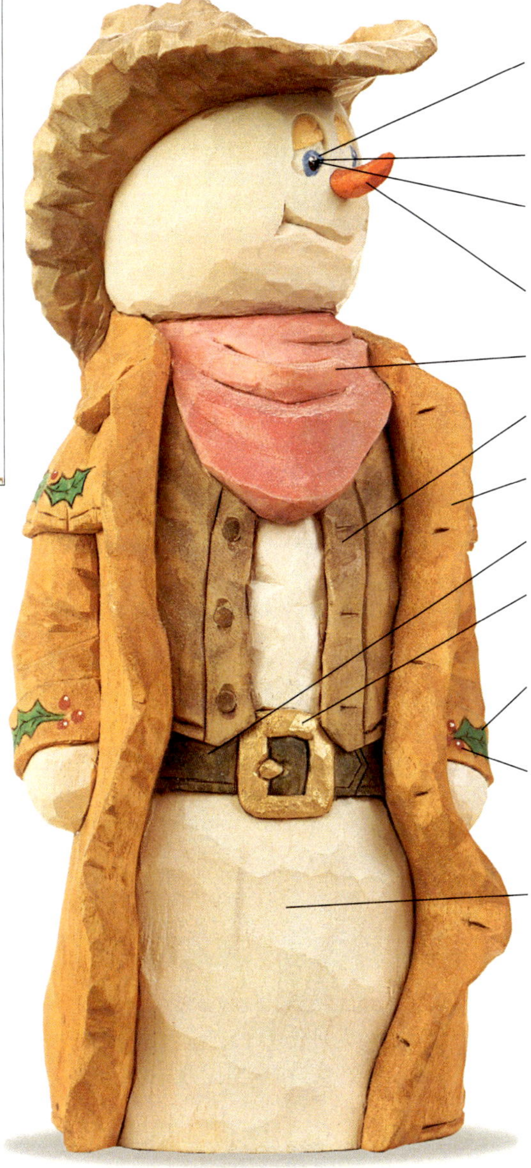

Iris: slightly thinned liberty blue (2)

Pupil: slightly thinned black (2)

Eye twinkle: titanium white (2) applied with point of toothpick

Carrot nose: orange (1)

Bandana: tompte red (2)

Vest, hat: burnt umber (2)

Coat: raw sienna (2)

Belt: black (2)

Buckle, coat buttons: slightly thinned kim gold (2)

Holly leaves: full-strength Christmas green (2)

Holly berries: Santa red (1) with tiny titanium white (2) dot on one side of each

Body, face: slightly thinned oyster white (2)

2 DecoArt Americana
3 Delta Ceramcoat

TIP

TO WASH OR NOT TO WASH?

Some carvers wash their woodcarving before painting, but I don't feel the need to do so. I, on the other hand, wash my hands several times a day while carving, and we wash our gloves regularly, so I always have a clean glove. I find that washing a carving with water makes the grain pop out and gives the carving a striped look, but you can seal your carving as desired.

Painting and Finishing

In the past, I've used wood bleach to make basswood white for snow, but the bleach can be difficult to find and challenging to use. So, we painted this snowman.

My wife, Barb, paints on the bare wood; we don't use any sort of sealer or base coat. When it comes to paint, we use whatever acrylic craft paint is on sale. Barb usually thins one or two drops of paint with a tablespoon of water.

Let the carving dry for at least one day. Then antique it. We mix equal parts boiled linseed oil and paint thinner. Brush the mixture on and allow it to dry for at least a day. Then seal it with one or two light coats of Deft satin finish.

materials & tools

MATERIALS:

- Basswood, 3" (7.6cm) thick: 3¼" x 7½" (8.3cm x 19.1cm)
- Acrylic paint, such as DecoArt Americana: orange, Santa red; such as Delta Ceramcoat: black, burnt umber, Christmas green, kim gold, liberty blue, oyster white, raw sienna, titanium white, tompte red
- Boiled linseed oil
- Paint thinner
- Finish, such as Deft satin
- Scotch-Brite® pad

TOOLS:

- Knives: bench; long thin-bladed
- Vise
- #3 palm gouge: 1" (25mm)
- #5 palm gouge: 1" (25mm)
- Large mallet-size gouge: 1" to 1½" (25mm to 38mm)
- Skew gouges, such as Flexcut
- V-tool (mallet-size): ⅜" to 7⁄16" (10mm to 11mm) 45°
- Rotary tool
- Woodburner with nib: writing
- Paintbrushes: assorted

The author used these products for the project. Substitute your choice of brands, tools, and materials as desired.

Snowman Clint Patterns

Gerald Sears and his wife, Barb, live on 20 acres in the Ozarks of the Southwest Missouri. The Sears have been carving and painting together for over 55 years. Gerald is a self-taught woodcarver and an original member of the Caricature Carvers of America. Barb, also self-taught, uses paints to breathe life into his characters. See more of their work at gnbsearswoodcarving.com.